Harvest of the Late Season

Harvest of the Late Season

Aniruddha Pathak

PARTRIDGE

A Penguin Random House Company

To order additional copies of this book, contact
Partridge India
000 800 10062 62
orders.india@partridgepublishing.com

www.partridgepublishing.com/india

Contents

Preface

Harvest of the late season, yes indeed it is. All my working life— ever since my days with the Times of India group of publications where I worked in the Economic Times during mid sixties— I only wrote analytical stuff for the newspaper. And later also when I shifted to the management side with the same company, and then through change of jobs this continued. Even when I retired, some of the periodicals requested me to continue to contribute articles regularly, which I initially thought, why not, but was difficult since I had decided also not to do the same thing I did all my working life. Yet, I was toying with the idea of continuing to write something. Only, that something was not spelt out, nor was I clear as to what.

The first thing I wanted to do with some time at my disposal was to read a few books that I had little time to read earlier. Bhagavad-Gita was one of them. I read a few interpretations available. No doubt they were scholarly without exception. But one thing that struck me was: they were too verbose for a song celestial so beautiful like Bhagavad-Gita, which no doubt is an excellent philosophical thought on way of life. Having said so, what is equally true, it is one of the best poetries in Sanskrit. This aspect was totally lost in all of the scholarly translations. Many of them were lost in explaining the words and expressions used. Well, analysis is the last thing one should do to any poetry. Further, what is left unsaid is often more significant than what is expressly said especially in poetry. Too much interpretation kills poetry. These things left me thinking.

And I decided to do my own translation— one, very brief and line to line, sticking to what is said without interpreting too much, allowing the reader to imagine on things left unsaid. Any way, right from my school days I insisted on understanding things in my own way and not too much on what the teacher explained in the classroom. No doubt my initial attempts (though they served my purpose) were far from satisfactory as a poetic translation. But I persevered. I must have redone my translation more than a dozen times since the year 2000 when I started off.

Simultaneously, I also began to read English poetry of which I had little exposure earlier. In a few years I started writing my own poems— almost laughable initially of course. I spent three-four years in this learning mode perhaps to reach a tolerable stage. Learning of course continues all through the life even for an accomplished poet. After Bhagavad-Gita I translated a few Upanishads, some work of Shankaracharya, Subhashitanis (words well said), and to end with Mahabharata where I selected over 2000 verses (shlokas) from the epic that has one hundred thousand verses. In addition I translated what I called Vyasa Ramayana (largely unknown to many— people know of Valmiki Ramayana and Tulsi Ramayana).

I also continued to write poems of my own in English, many of which are on a website (PoemHunter.com). It was through this website that I was in touch with Partridge Publishers and hence this book.

As to the contents this compilation includes about 370 poems. They are divided in six chapters as shown. Yet, the classification is largely arbitrary. All sonnets are included in one along with villanelles, although some of them can easily be included under Spirituality, or even as humour. The same is true about poems under Musings as well as Miscellany. A poem has many dimensions in theme and nature. It has many nuances. Yet, all said and done a poem is what the reader interprets. Once delivered, it loses its address. And the reader is the best judge.

I must acknowledge here the contributions of a few persons that made my task easier. My own exposure to Sanskrit was limited to whatever I learned at the school. Later, with a lot of reading, I built up good vocabulary in Sanskrit. Two good dictionaries: one, Sanskrit to English by Vaman S Apte, and another, English to Sanskrit by M Moneier Williams were of tremendous help. To this was added the help from my wife who is a graduate in Sanskrit. I must also acknowledge help from my brother-in-law, a physician and cancer specialist by profession, and one who also has contributed in the field of literature.

As for poems as such I must mention here tremendous support and encouragement received from my elder brother who comes from a different discipline— a doctorate in Economics. He read my stuff which I am sure was not so interesting to read at the early stage, telling me still that he liked it and that I must continue. He also gave me several books apart from literature from Internet, not only the soft version but a hard copy duly filed into folders and indexed. He even got me lap-top and other paraphernalia to make my task easier. If my poems are on a website, PoemHunter.com, the credit goes to him for putting them there— for, poems have to be uploaded one by one, title, text, sub-text, classification, and what not, which requires good amount of patience that I lack.

This harvest of late season, as it were, is here in the form of a compilation of poems. I hope the readers would like this labour of love of a late evening.

Aniruddha Pathak

Sonnets, Villanelles

Contents

Never the root cause

Man, since time woke from a long pause,
Has chased everything but the root—
A trait that can sniff no right cause
In his ways anxious for fair fruit:
Cavemen first blamed spirits evil,
Witch doctors dabbled with vile will,
And vaidyas[1], game doshas[2] to blame,
Blamed, body's not in balanced frame,
Or, not in good alignment are
The planets with what's ruling star,
Now, nor ever, man matched his creed:
Seeds sown bear fruits, as does man's deed.
    And look at me oft blaming mood,
    Not, I've miles to go to be good.

---

1. Vaidyas[1]: Ayurvedic doctors in India
2. Doshas[2]: three bodily fault lines, blemishes

- Sonnets | 01.12.14 |

1

No use in shallows to swim

Li'le do we know how in this world to wind:
Name nor yet fame we fall for gems-jewels,
Knowing well, mundane shine lasts for brief spells,
Who heeds his heart? Head's busy faults to find;
Who cares right from wrong, truth showing its hue?
Knowing well, eyes can't facts from falsehood find,
From red rags reasons— sound from ill-designed,
Who'd know to wind in this world if not you?
It is no use still in shallows to swim,
Perchance we know well: truths far deeper dwell,
It's scratching of conscience truth to tell,
Stir still, from depth does surface crème o' crème.
　　The day we wake up, be the dawn of life,
　　A journey starts thence of unknown births rife.

_____

- Sonnets | 03.12.14 |

Rejoice, the soul is alive

Should the sight of star-spangled skies at night
Drench you deep with wonderment of a child,
And that of blue skies, with the same delight,
And if this unknown joy be no less wild;
If a blade of grass springing up in field,
And a bud blossoming into young flower,
Both move you no less still with untold power;
If age has none of your child's wonder killed;
If nature's plainest things pose a message
That lingers long in your memories isled,
If your child lives young every passing age,
At no time are his wonders reconciled;
 File reason not in use and remain naïve,
 Divide your age by a factor of five,
 Rejoice; your soul and child both are alive!

This sonnet allows itself one extra line.

- Sonnets | 15.12.14 |

A duet sung alone

Now I know how confusing was to find—
I loved my love walking a one-way street,
Not knowing what her heart willed, not one whit,
Chaotic sure was it, bit cuter kind,
For, silent came my love, clueless the same,
Though frost with unknown chill, warm still no end,
A strange seed sprouting on a plant sans name,
Love building nest, hard was to comprehend;
A nest was it, not yet by one bird made,
Was built for two, reinforced to last long,
With a plinth-stone so precious as of jade;
For a while I lone sang a duet song,
> *She had the same frustration that I felt,*
> *Love frost for long thence on began to melt.*

- Sonnets | 02.10.14 |

Blest be to earn your pardon

My green mood-maker, no grief to him grim,
Heralding breeze of good days wafting near,
The heart he had my wails of woes to hear,
Howso brief his visits my life's sole dream;
And this time too I was looking forward
To meeting, to making my dull life bright,
Excited, eager, fleeting, felt like bird,
In plight still, li'le could I sleep the long night;
Yet, came the breeze, passed by, not a leaf moved,
He came to town and left— not meeting me,
And I knew not how much or if he loved.
O deep sea, let no cloak in closet be,
*   Nor live nor can I die, huge be this burden,*
*   Let me know; I'd feel blest to earn your pardon.*

- Sonnets | 01.09.14 |

5

In the lap of storms

Slumped off we never sit, nor breathe easy,
On reaching home shores nor in content coo,
Nor crow we struggled hard at stormy sea,
Just that we shed sour sweat, goals to pursue.
And on kissing the goal, in fair tides rise,
Like naught else joys of success weigh in world,
Yet, resting in peace we doubt if be wise,
For, made are we of clay as yet un-stirred;
To pray for things to ease is not our mark,
Nor compromises with hardship to make,
We look the storm in face and call its lark,
In troubled waters, devils do we rake.
  It's not in us to breathe hollow at home,
  Strange joys jostle us in the lap of storm.

- Sonnets | 03.09.14 |

Life and happiness

Way back bare a child I'd as many joys
As wonders wandered in my wanton worlds,
And joys when jingled along sundry toys,
I felt, was a tad happier than birds.
Came youth, what changed were not but childhood toys,
Rewards of life innocent nigh no more,
Boys chasing girls, and girls giggly at boys,
Till maturity moose knocked at the door;
My earthen pot kept in kiln to ripen,
Life's realities reeling hard and keen,
Old happiness failing to enliven,
And I was nudged to kneel, to look within.
*   In fond hope more fulfilling life to find;*
*   Isn't life leaving blasé ecstasies behind?*

- Sonnets | 08.09.14 |

Times two wear hard on me

You promised seasons-like, assured me
You'd sure come, was lost still awaiting—
A ship-wrecked for rescue at mid-sea,
But seldom can words give fair inkling.
Not so brave to live thru times of scare,
Vexed was I: what if you still can't come—
Troubles and strife turn up from nowhere,
Caught in, what if you can't make it home?

I thence lapsed into what when you leave,
If at all or when you'd come again,
Worse than death, scarce can you this believe,
And e'er since, a wreck I feel in pain.
    Times only two wear hard every eve,
    Ere you come and time 'tis when to leave.

One lost in love gets lost in thoughts waiting for his belovéd who was
expected as per date and time fixed earlier. The sonnet is set in nine
syllabic anapaest metre, not the usual iambic penta-metre.

- Sonnets | 02.08.14 |

Head and heart both

Let rocky dead intellect go its way,
Logic of do's and don'ts, let them all lie,
The rules of grammar gathered yesterday,
Metres and feet are best looked askance nigh.
Flow from aside, o'er them, and go ahead,
Let melody get born from notes of noise,
Listening not but to the inner voice,
You flow ahead, by heart over head led.
In purest form, in its simplest so far,
Like a perennial river flows poem,
None of a starry string, it's a lone star,
One that pretends to be no studded gem!

Gone ahead as said, this is what got made—
A product still of heart as much as head!

A poem flows like a river. Intellect with its do's and don'ts often is like rocks and stones blocking river's flow. But when it flows ahead still despite them, music is born.

A poem is always a product of heart to start with as I know. The heart may have reasons unknown to head. A stage still comes when head slowly takes over. Yet, creativity comes from the chaos created by heart, the source of all poems! And yet alas there is no escaping head.

- Sonnets | 10.08.14 |

The gift of tears

A lot is lost—losses unheard,
And still have saved a price-less thing—
A stream of tears easy that spring,
By women of this wanton world;
A lot is saved, things nigh weird—
Position and power and prestige,
High walls to hold women in siege,
By man-folk of very same world;
And yet, gains regained at grave cost:
The greatest gift of God to cry,
Shedding tears nor making eyes moist,
And art of making heart lighter nigh!
    And reason why his heart is brittle cake,
      No lunch laid free for wanton a man's sake!

- Sonnets | 19.08.14 |

A poet and river

A stream I'm struggling O with tears,
Blocked on way by many an odd stone,
And wonder how to move on my own,
How to flow unhindered free from fears.

A poet I am singing my heart,
To heart cleave, in heart do I believe,
To heads still devil's due do I give,
Two pillars and placed still poles apart!

An endless duel raging within,
What I wish to say wilts yon of words,
Words are still all 'pon which I must lean,
Words and words, all wearing wings of birds,
    A quenchless quench, dilemma of life,
    No way still but walking edge-of-knife!

This piece uses a nine-syllabic (three feet) anapaest metre unlike most sonnets that use ten-syllabic (five feet) iamb.

- Sonnets | 21.08.14 |

Be thy own light

In many a scripture I read,
Divergent delve the varied views,
The world's wise various in their creed,
My wisdom weighs me to confuse.
Hindu monks choose saffron to wear,
The Buddhists come in their yellow,
All-white is what Jainis1 prefer,
And some wear none but their halo,
All contrive to clot my keen mind.
Whose word of wisdom to follow?
Who can help me heaven to find?
Who, my here-aft, oh whereso I go?
  Not else than thine atman's within,
  And be thou thine own light serene.

---

1. Jainis: Jain **shvetāmbar** sect wears white robes. The other called **digambar** believes that dimensions represent their garments and wear nothing.

Anand was Buddha's closest disciple. Seeing his master breathing his last, he felt a void without his guru's guiding spirit. It is then that Buddha uttered his last words: 'O be thou thine own light.' It is said that Anand contemplated on these words and realised true knowledge within 24 hours of Buddha's death.

- Sonnets | 22.08.14 |

A fossil and seed

A fossil once there was of tree,
In layers of tradition wrapt—
Layers that proved, and proof well kept,
Yet, that was scarce its cause to be,
Of living in now's sole moment,
In hopes of unfolding morrow;
For, fossil was a force all spent,
Potential, nor seed that can grow;
But when chose to blossom as seed,
And be one day a tree well grown,
Flowers and fruits as promised creed,
And ripe possibilities prone!
    A seed soaked sooner might well sprout,
    A fossil would have frost in doubt.

- Sonnets | 23.08.14 |

Sculpting poems

Stripped down to core, brought to the barest bone,
The chipping-chopping of a sculptor,
Probing the heart of a huge chunk of stone,
In search of a vaguely hinted figure,
Be poet's chipping of churning vague thoughts,
Imagining how the mused lady looks,
Linking up like a child the dotted dots,
Yet, it's no cooking from recipe books;
The sculptor's strokes of love might silent speak,
The poet's pampered words might as well sing,
And metered or not, rhythm their own seek,
Each reader then wings in his own meaning.
>   *Oft yet, chipped and chopped on a thankless day,*
>   *The lady seems to tell: O there's no way!*

- Sonnets | 01.07.14 |

E'en dogs die no dog's death

As one born in freedom, to my life blest,
I dream, free-will I've earned my death to choose,
To die in ease divine— if nigh in haste,
That, froth of my fermenting flesh I lose.
So, in a hospice of a hospital
Of choice, prepare I to welcome my death,
That I make my journey's end beautiful,
As death, as always, is my fervent faith.
As lived I've this life through to ripe old age,
And keen am now to rid this garment grim,
As did many an ancient seer and sage;
And barking dogs then woke me from my dream.
    Pray, man I'm, scarce can live a life canine,
    Don't I deserve merciful death benign?

I often imagine myself in this situation— an old man on deathbed,
suffering and pleading for a merciful death in peace— euthanasia.

- Sonnets | 03.07.14 |

Art is no milch cow

What if Mona Lisa's treated like corn?
In multiple forms made and marketed,
From one of a kind and mysterious born,
That steals a wondrous heart and turns keen head.
Imagine several shades of dull grey,
Epics that go on, never showing ends,
A race ran in endless rounds of relay,
A bouquet that brags big till blossom bends.
Art's art but if captured in compact space,
And least if stretched on and on till it yawns,
Nor if fattened in self-love, lacking grace,
Nor o'er-Indulged like wild-grown garden lawns;
    Art's no cow milked and marketed to death,
    Mysterious be mapped not in one swell breath.

In response to commercialisation and mass production of master pieces like Mona Lisa.

- Sonnets | 06.07.14 |

Tides and troubles wait for none

Kneeling under the vault of open sky,
I bent down trying to reach the wet sand,
A fragment of swept-ashore shell in hand,
And wrote upon a patch nigh wind-swept dry—
Whatso that came cascading in high gear,
And walked away ne'er once to turn, look back
At weary words wilting my mental deck,
I knew the tide was closing in to clear.

There followed truth in all its driving force:
Cathartic quite 'tis penning down one's pain,
And cure, to every trouble on the course,
Like rain ending a lingering hot reign!
    In every tide its counter's sure espied,
    A waxing tide a waning one doth hide.

- Sonnets | 07.07.14 |

Time to scale down

Tonnes of glitter and gloss gasping to race
Up the runway, rising to kiss the sky,
Lifted bare by lean air, pumping up pace,
Or else lands lower down from heavens high,
And with a puff of smoke and sticky squeal,
Touches the tarmac tamely 'pon soft wheels,
And brain and brawn in boast man much proud feels.
Yet, birds when bid better it's no big deal,
Forgetting, their big birds gulp wells of fuel,
Shatter ears, silent while true angels fly,
Tanked up on just fruity nectar, et al,
Shaming e'en fighter pilots, mute in sigh;
    And little housefly scarce can help but laugh:
    Dog fights? Watch us do that and more by half!

We all as kids have spent hours watching in disbelief planes fly, take off and land. No doubt, we have also marvelled at the birds doing all that with consummate ease. But only when we grow up do we realise how well the birds do so as compared to the best of flying machines. And yet, most flying insects also do this and more even better than birds, and go unnoticed still!

Men have put all their bets in scaling up technology. Only of late has he focused on scaling down, perhaps inspired by microbes. This sonnet was born from this fascination.

- Sonnets | 01.06.14 |

Jades from jacinth and gems

Like mapping a stranger from not a scratch,
When from a given menu you've to get':
A latest pair of shoes and socks that match,
An elegantly designed suit, a set
Of cuff-links that propagate packaged myth,
All of which pronounce peripheral him,
Diving deep lone may let what lies beneath,
It takes patience ere rises up the cream.
The same perhaps is true for a poem,
Yet, how many the patience spare to reach
Up to jewels from the hallowed ho hum,
Yet, who likes depths of sea from fancied beach?
    And even there from amongst pearls of them,
    It's hard judging jades from jacinth of gem.

This sonnet is born of a dilemma: There are scores of poems to choose from. No doubt there are jacinth and gems among them. But there too are jades as are artificial stones. And there is too little time, too brief an attention span, and competing diversions galore.

- Sonnets | 02.06.14 |

How I felt seeing my son

Curious and anxious in some hopes of heaven,
Felt I seeing the face of my first joy,
Half hoping to see daughter, much less son,
I entered spring in steps, heart in some buoy,
And scanned the feeble face of infancy,
Peering at the four pounds, packaged thrill wrapped—
A long awaited bliss, rare ecstasy
Was in arms, and felt fatherhood on tap.
Yet found little imprint of hers, nor mines,
There are things too far for a man to see,
Still harder to see subtle tell-tale signs,
Yet, every drop has an imprint of sea.
> *'They come like that and no less darling still',*
> *I heard her say, and felt a guilty chill.*

-Sonnets | 05.06.14 |

Disillusion is when bliss

If life's naught but energies that vibrate,
An if what vibrates as well makes some sound,
If or not can man grasp it or translate,
A strange matrix of sounds world's all around.
Yet, if the world is not but illusion,
Vain it seems to search for its warp and whoop,
Meaning, nor purpose of all the motion,
Lest he get caught in a deluding loop,
That the wise of world call disillusion;
Ah, what a serendipity it be,
Disillusion, spiritual inversion,
And bliss, other worldly and heavenly!
*   An if death every illusion destroys,*
*   Ah, what a friend 'tis fetching blissful joys!*

If the phenomenal world is nothing but Maya, an illusion, a man who is disillusioned with worldly life sees the truth. The only time he seems to be in sense. And in a final Volta, the sonnet says: death, if it destroys all illusions, is the greatest friend, no foe.

- Sonnets | 07.06.14 |

The beauty in you is you

If wondrous most thing about world be world,
The beauteous most a thing in you is you.
I see this clearer now e'en with eyes blurred,
As soon or late truth always gets its due;
You might not this believe though borne by heart,
Which, today's men of mall-turned robots lack,
Yet, heart's all there's to hail if mart be art,
So, with not else but heart let me this crack,
(I know, I aught deal with women as are,
(And never once how I'd like them to be,
(There's but one way if man wants to go far:
(Call a puddle not just pond, a vast sea!)
    So, everything 'bout you is doubtless beau,
    Yet, the most beauteous spot in you is you.

- Sonnets (tongue-in-cheek) | 08.06.14 |

Mea culpa

Man is made to beware of destiny,
Yet, deep down I'm what driving desire is,
As is desire so be my 'will' and me,
So are designed my deeds, so be my bliss,
Ah deeds, destiny's greatest, greenest lea,
Rejoice I still should fate bring me 'fair' cheers,
Bemoan should the same fate bring 'unfair' tears,
Yet, fortune nor fate, man 'lone is mighty,
'I' should foretell how my life I should lead,
Not stars whose own destiny's not set in stone,
None of whom knows from what soil's cast its bone.
An if fortune favours the seed called deed,
    And this seed grows in soil garnished with now,
    Strange, I still blame my destiny somehow.

- Sonnets | 01.05.14 |

When you pressed me to pen a poem

When you pressed me to pen a piece—a few
Good lines the least for a well-meaning friend,
And soon to leave, it left me starring blue
Skies, blinking stars, and blank paper in hand,
Which, soon turned to brooding on things and ways,
Poems are no stray gifts picked from shelved piles,
Nor can I spell nor parrot a vain praise;
And words and lines receded far by miles.
Perhaps, had you been just daughter, you see—
Not one with an escape loop of '-in-law',
Would I have fished out one as if from sea?
The fruit of my fishing I doubt you saw—
A piece penned a daughter-in-law to please,
For which I'd heart nor head her to displease.

Why can't a daughter-in-law be a daughter? Rhetorical, yet, easier said than tried to make it happen. From this dilemma has this sonnet been born.

- Sonnets | 08.05.14 |

Let me keep my illusion

Her face to me means freshness of green lea,
Her eyes inviting tempts me to explore,
And bosom brings warmth to life oft wintry—
All-weather port beckoning me ashore;
Each acre of her fine anatomy,
Belittled and maligned as mortal flesh
That would one day be one with dust or ash,
Or face of Maya if not enemy,
All this the least in me dimmest lamp lit,
For me, I'd rather in unlit dark live,
In search of strange solace if illusive;
Let all keep philosophy's high spirit,
    To me life is immortal as is death,
    Illusive though, I'd keep in her my faith.

- Sonnets | 01.04.14 |

Man that hath too much mind . . .

I've not one flower with a drawn face seen,
Nor yet bird calling an unhappy tune,
Nor oak worried, vague on losing her green,
A dolphin depressed, nor despairing moon,
A reindeer delving on his self esteem,
A polar bear that can't take it easy,
Nor a wild cat worried of her fond dream;
No, they live life as it unfolds to be.

And seen I've cats practising peaceful Zen,
Ducks meditating while floating in ease;
He that has too much mind seems only man,
Who, never once at peace be whatso is,
Violated who has, poisoned Ma Earth,
Polluting still, and plundering her worth.

- Sonnets | 03.04.14 |

I look at greens of my life's grey garden

I watch Madhu Maltee bloom in my garden—
Long fingered flowers, some red, some still white,
The reds born in light and the whites at night,
Deprived of day light and warmth of the sun,
Which, 'pon begetting day's sun to red turn,
Unlike ripe age whose red turns to dull grey,
Lost that has child's sense of now one sad day,
In growing old, ah grey wisdom to earn.
These flowers, like all greens perhaps, do know
The value of now unlike human kind,
Who, to Nature's gift, passing moment blind,
Lives on time lost, hollow dreams to follow;
 Wizened of late, I watch greens grow in awe,
 In wonder, how it feels feeling the now!

- Sonnets | 05.04.14 |

Life and death and fear

Two owls came and sat 'pon a branch beside,
One with a snake caught in its crooked beak,
Its companion, a mouse from close by creek,
Both them awaiting death, had not yet died,
Lusting for mouse, the snake forgot its death,
Such has in food every life's fervent faith.

Seeing the snake the mouse, too fraught with fear,
Nigh well forgot, gasping it was for breath,
And both the owls mighty mystified were:
It's fear of death! Ah greater dread than death!
Though part of life dies everyday unseen,
Man's scared only when death's seen, felt within.

Yet, more one curses death, more kisses life,
More he lusts life, more is filled with fears rife.

- Sonnets | 04.02.14 |

Keep no monkey at bay

Discoursing said a learned man of grade:
Fear and fight sin, be not man of thick skin;
A mendicant, long silent protested—
Stop this sense slaughter and sink in your sin.
The learned man, aghast, stopped his discourse
And mused: what a mantra: Sink unto sin!
And asked: I've got the cart, pray, where's the horse?
This, this: Seek thy solace from what has been,
Beware ne'er yet to think of old monkey.
Yet, hard it is to keep monkeys at bay,
More one tries to miss more they mar the play;
The man much tried, and hit 'pon this prized key:
> *Fight nor fear sin, nor run 'way from the scene,*
> *Let witness watch from wings— involved, nor keen.*

Yet, naught whatso alas is easy in life— letting the witness, your atman to watch! All man can do is to try, I too. Perhaps, it is easier than keeping the monkey at bay.

- Sonnets | 05.02.14 |

To learn from every turn

A spring prevails forever, nor green reign,
From grass I try to learn some persistence,
From trees the value of quiet patience,
No winter's wellness withers in all vain,
If eyes I have, if I have ears to learn,
No garden is by winter too deterred,
Nor yet by spring is unduly flattered,
And Nature teaches me at every turn
That goodness springs from every evil heart,
Summer there is, I learn, in all winter,
And winter in the heart of all summer,
Evil is frost in good if seen apart;
    So I care spring nor autumn, good nor ill,
    If I can learn from Nature's turning wheel.

- Sonnets | 05.01.14 |

Pain, infant's first gain

Would this pain to eternal life transform?
Yea, bow down to pain, humble and bent-head,
Hopeless now, it'd one day be potent norm,
Its touch transforming buds to blossoms red,
Let every pain to its tallest crest cling,
Moving on matters more than journey's end,
Take troubles to their ultimate unfolding,
Means are no less meaningful than the end.
And art of life is not avoiding pain1—
Nor is pain's predominance o'er pleasure2
Punishment— perhaps endurance raiser,
It's pain perhaps, mankind stays somewhat sane;
  Or else, why should a new born suffer pain?
  Why's he delivered? Pain's infant's first gain.

---

1. The art of life is the avoidance of pain.
   – Thomas Jefferson, To Mrs Cosway, 1786
2. The preponderance of pain over pleasure is the cause of our fictitious morality and religion.
   – Friedrich Nietzsche, The Antichrist

- Sonnets | 06.01.14 |

And I turned in my sleep for the nth time

My mind had from a million alts to choose:
To marvel beauty of the moonless sky,
To re-live that meandering slow cruise,
Sweet waft from her lithe reclined self nearby,
Or of the bluebell blossoms of late springs;
I could have dwelt at her demur most dimple
That seems to dig deeper whenso she sings,
Robbing my sleep; could have delved at her ample
Bosom— any pleasant thought of the time;
But worries weighed in, crowding out my joys.
I wonder how the head holds on to grime
More than dwelling on dreams, life's bliss and buoys;
    And reasoning with me with no good rhyme,
    I twisted in bed, turned for the nth time.

- Sonnets | 01.02.13 |

Cooking up budgets

The halwa1 cooked we hope is sweeter made,
Flavoured with sops and served with a straight face,
That our household hisaab2, high, inflated,
May at last recover its long lost grace;
The budget-cooks, (no, not crooks, too unkind,
Uncouth), harder placed are sweetness to find,
And as proof of pudding slowly does grind,
They pass on ripe fruit with its bitter rind.

The top chef then comes lacing witty lines,
Poetic quotes palatable to make
It, while poor tithe payer in patience dines
On a stale loaf of bread that looks like cake.
    A fine recipe pretending to bake
    Cake, seeking whilst safe electoral stake!

---

1. Halwa[1]: The code word used by bureaucrats for budget preparations. Halwa is a popular sweet dish in India.
2. Hisaab[2]: Hindi for accounts of income and outgo being kept by middle class families every month.

-Sonnets | 03.02.13 |

Coveting

In a world ever-the-more-wanting seized,
And yet, with more and more less and less pleased,
Potholed, pitted by marginal returns,
To that pot of profusion lead when tracks,
Truth paying tithe to logic that it lacks,
And wanting to coveting in time turns,
There's vulture1 in man, contentment diseased.

And should demand fall, greed getting to grind,
The learned lot lamenting recession,
The world should still well off feel to my mind,
A universal cooling of hot passion,
Of burning red greed, blinding blasé desire,
That fueled markets to a raging fire,
I'd scarce yet too much of trouble there find.

---

1. Vulture represents greed, which perhaps comes from **gṛdha**, meaning to covet, greed. From this comes **giḍha**, vulture, in Hindi.

This sonnet has an atypical rhyming and stanza scheme.

- Sonnets | 04.04.13 |

The four that think of me

Men of four minds worship me in this world,
The Lord said in divine Song Celestial,
Three of them bring along a begging bawl
And feel: veiled whispers of wants would be heard.
One comes suffering body-mind borne pain,
The second comes wanting money and means,
The third a curious bird, knowledge to gain,
Their prayer with pleads and pardons begins.

There's one that feels: belief in God is odd,
Man of science seeks to know the unknown,
And one e'en called a long missing myth 'God'!
And fourth loves me for love's sake, one alone,
Wishes he has nor wants; seeks nor does search,
And finds in me an ever-lasting perch!

In Bhagavad-Gita (verses 7.16-18), Krishna tells Arjun: there are four kinds of men that come to me. He called them **ārti**, **arthārthi**, **jijñā su**, and **jñāni**. The first two types we come across on a daily basis. The third type are also not far to seek. A recent example was that of a scientist calling his illusive sub-atomic particle a God particle. The Lord said, 'I love them all, for, they at least approach me; but I love the last one the most. He loves me for love's sake'.

- Sonnets | 12.04.13 |

Earth Day

In days of Vedas man prayed for the earth
That he enjoyed the joys of Nature's bliss
Wounding none her welfare nor ever worth,
He who's killed her today with greed of his,
Audacious, pretends still her to please,
Dedicating a mere day1— of all things,
Forgetting still, the jack of fool that he's,
That everything but from planet earth springs.
Oblivious, he's here on a short lease,
From her womb has he hailed, there would return,
Life looks good long as her goodness green is,
Ere she dies due man-made sins, be his turn.
    Mortally wounded, she's bleeding today,
    Too little, too late seems alas Earth Day.

---

1.   Dedicating a day to earth: Man forgets that days and nights happen only because the earth rotates around her axis. So, every single day dawns thanks to her. Who is he to allot a day to her and pretend he has done enough for her?

Thoughts on International Earth Day: 22nd April.

- Sonnets | 14.04.13 |

A cat dead and alive!

Where awareness walks wearing no illusion,
And head is held high, where knowledge is free,
And truth is one whole taking no division,
To such a heaven Lord do let me be.

Illusion an alt ID be for world,
Knowledge a weapon to wield, power to build,
Truth seldom hailed one whole—this or that bird,
A part looking like whole fetching full yield,
The twain dancing under shadowy light,
As mind be-muddled with this or that lore,
Seeing things black or else white, wrong or right,
Awhile truth's stuck on a far distant shore.

Good grace, world has photons1 that better know—
Living dual life at once: matter and moa[2]!

---

1. Photon has the ability to be simultaneously present at two places, has incredible awareness to mutate from a wave (energy) to particle (matter). A quantum mystery, an either-or dichotomy! Mind suffers from this-or-that paradigm: wave or particle, day or night, sad or happy, black or white . . . Often a part makes more sense than the whole. A jigsaw puzzle incomprehensible when complete! Computer accepts 0 or 1. Human mind is not much better. On the other hand, holistic awareness is non-dual awareness, the undifferentiated whole.
2. Moa is an extinct NZ bird. Here it means, when matter exists (its opposite energy or wave) is extinct, and vice versa.

This sonnet goes on a wonderment trip on the wings of these facts.

- Sonnets | 01.05.13 |

Gold standard

Coffers may be spilling with gold and jade—
Precious pearls and treasure troves, you said?
A loaf of bread still makes for better aid
To a hungry maw thereby happy made.

If everyone talks of the priceless gold,
What price thence be its price tag, what price cost,
Should all sing of its value manifold?
Gold standard is fat man's toast, vainest boast.

And greed for gold me seems is not for gold,
Nor yet silver, that has not yet glittered;
Perhaps, promise vague precious metals hold—
A promise posted, not yet delivered.

Pity be to man of material mould
That would want his dreams to glitter with gold.

- Sonnets | 05.05.13 |

Voyage of wonder

The first time when the man was made to see:
No more Mother Earth, Sun our centre is,
That, planets ply 'round Sun, not what he sees,
His belief's sole ship sank, bottomed at sea.
Aught he learn once again: no mere body,
He's soul within— a long lost truth so sound,
The truth forgotten in his long journey,
The truth sages for ages made profound:
More than man a spiritual being he's,
That happens to live today human life,
A luminous thing of love, light, and bliss,
No sack of flesh and bones, intellect rife,
    Set out on an endless voyage of wonder,
    To discover yet higher thrills of thunder!

French Jesuit Pierre Teilhard de Chardin propounded a new paradigm of spiritual thought on man's true identity: 'We are not human beings having a spiritual experience. We are spiritual beings having a human experience.'

This paraphrases what our ancient sages said in various Upanishads in so many ways and words: that man's truer identity is his atman— his spiritual self; the body is just a vehicle for the soul within. This soul constantly yearns for a spiritual voyage to discover higher planes. Today man has forgotten that he is not a body with soul, but soul with a body as vehicle—a vehicle for his voyage of wonder.

- Sonnets | 01.06.13 |

If man were to make his exit

No life has a mind that can match with mine,
Nor can produce work of art, nor yet speech,
Nor music nor poetry so divine;
I alone have the reach O rare to reach;
Violating a while his womb of birth,
Taking more than he gives, growth in disguise,
A vulture wanting ever more from earth,
So the man thinks, clever, crooked than wise.

If wiser were he than the rest of life,
No proof supporting has he proffered still,
Prescribing placebos of a progress pill
That would one day prove death warrants1 of strife
    To earth, who'd sure heave a sigh of relief,
    Were a man to make an exit soon if.

---

1.   Death warrants: It alludes to the challenges the planet faces today, like misuse of natural resources: unsafe drinking water, toxin-tainted food, polluted air, climate of extremes, frequent and unnatural disasters, low immunity and new diseases, declining quality of life, rise in greed and ethical dilemmas and conflicts, and many more.

- Sonnets | 02.06.13 |

The death of a word

A word oft gets picked first by a poet,
Or by a penster turning goodly prose,
Which, awhile lives happy without much let,
Fresh and fragrant ah like a high-breed rose;
The word for a while wandering still young,
Unburdened by a foot-loose man's baggage,
As fresh as came say from a foreign tongue,
But all things alive and naught still, soon age.

The wordsmiths1 of world when get hold of it,
Chewing it— dog as does a piece of bone,
Twisting it in time, bit by tedious bit
Till it flashes odd hews never ere known.
   Poor little word gasps for precious breath,
   Alive, yet dying a premature death!

---

1. Wordsmiths: It alludes to media men and sundry journalists, so busy meeting deadlines with breaking news that they have no time to watch the words they use.

- Sonnets | 03.06.13 |

Books more durable are

Books, testaments of wit, shrines of fine learning,
Edifices, far more hard-wearing are
Than those in stones built by sword's might of power,
Some by Papal decree were set a burning.
Books, besides, have to be resilient more:
Look at old wisdom standing still robust,
Letters intact, whose syllables still soar,
Stones, temples all have been while done to dust.

For every page of a book burnt in rage,
For every book's past lost by flame in shame,
More words escape than thought of from each page,
O to rise later like phoenix from flame.

And yet he that slays men mars God's image,
He that burns books blights His very visage.

- Sonnets | 04.06.13 |

In favour of books

No such thing's known as moral of a book,
Character might there be though of a crook,
Yet, as there be a good, not so good cook,
As there's well-done dish, books do tempt re-look.

The books that a notorious name beget,
Open up to world their well-hidden ill,
Those that make readers ill, seldom market
Well; yet, few books do grave public evil.

As no one book can all of wisdom boast—
Let it be rarest of prophetic art,
Cities may be sacked and books burned to roast1,
The thirst for truth, for freedom, rears in heart.

Books that red rags to powers raise rage a battle[2],
Challenging ones awhile reigning powers rattle.

---

1. Alludes to what Omar said at the capture of Alexandria, quoted by Emerson:
   'Burn the literature, for their value is in this one book (the Koran)'.
2. From Alfred Whitney, Essays on Education:
   'A book may be as great a thing as a battle.'

- Sonnets | 05.06.13 |

Search for truth

It seldom goes easy— the search for truth,
For, few can fathom an infinite whole,
It can't be too hard still, I thought in youth,
Let me not miss truth's universal soul;
Every endeavour adds to new knowledge,
Each effort put in paints her fair image;
And no one scales steep slopes of truth in vain,
Every climb helps one reach a greater height,
Each step helps one morrow's height to attain,
Not truth if, every search gains newer light.
I knew not still, few truths may breathe deep breath
Of reason, for creature truth is of faith.
    Like most dreamers in their early raw youth,
    I too mistook my illusion as truth.

- Sonnets | 06.06.13 |

Mind be when no good maid

My heart like an open palm is —no fist,
There's no secret whatso that I should hide,
I've said what I know leaving naught the least,
Yet, have ye grasped all height, its heft so wide?
Clouds may drain out all water in their hold,
A pot still not placed prime shall scarce get filled,
So seems the subtle wisdom told, retold,
It's not enough pots are placed in right field,
Yet, but he who's rightly inclined receives;
A fresh water stream flows in from a hill,
One with parched throat must partake what it gives,
So should what's said strike sense to keen ears still.
*   And there are things that scarce in words be said—*
*   The voice of heart's yon mind, mind's no good maid.*

Gautam Buddha and his disciple Anand were walking through a quiet wood whose solitude and silence prompted Anand to ask a question that for a long time was struggling to find expression: After you became buddha, you have been discoursing virtually non-stop on many occult subjects, and answering to our queries. I want to know if you have said all that you have to say. Have you come across people who really understand what you say? This poem imagines what Buddha might have said.

- Sonnets | 08.06.13 |

45

O to know me

Asked once to introduce who I'm— in short
At a workshop, to me a tall demand,
My thoughts took me to wonderful new port:
Who hast him ever known that I'd, my friend?
Closest he dwells in heart, yet far from shore,
A close friend he's or damnedest of a foe,
Witness to all my thoughts and acts my door,
A stranger still, an unknown Jill or Joe!
Body's to him a tooth brush—use and throw,
Mind, a monkey—out and eager to trick,
Amidst them as a walking-beating stick,
The 'I' must struggle to evolve and grow.
*   Not 'I', but an impostor sure I know,*
*   He that struts around calling him ego!*

- Sonnets | 09.06.13 |

He alone is happy

He whose health longer lives, as lives his cash,
Than life and limbs last, cheer jolly long years,
He that suffers no ill, whose laugh's like flash,
He that recalls goodly fate, has few fears,
He, whose worries to heavens have been lent,
Haply whose ego would climb down from hills,
Work to him is worship, not fruits fragrant,
In neighbour joys he who his own heart fills,
He that can live in this present moment,
Whose past has died, and future's not yet born,
Whose face smiles, mind muses, heart has no dent,
Living in Lent, looks forward to next morn.
    Such strange souls, faceless few, are far afar,
    Not on this earth, may live on far off star!

Few truly know what happiness is. But if pressed, would make a long list of what according to them happiness may be. As most things are in this world, happiness too suffers from duality. It is a two-sided coin. Pain and pleasure, day and night, light and dark, good and evil, one cannot exist without its opposite.

In the first twelve lines of this poem a bucket list is made. But to find a man answering to all the conditions happiness we will have to perhaps go beyond this earth to a heavenly star! The mood of the poem is tongue-in-cheek light.

- Sonnets | 10.06.13 |

To build a happy house of sands

If half my happiness should hail from cradle—
Be it peacock's monsoon dance, cuckoo's coo,
Be it a frugal meal's caressing taste,
Retiring or rising sun at seashore,
Reassuring touch of love lost in time,
Fragrance of beloved's flesh fresh from toilet;
And half, from what happens to life in saddle,
Not from how it unfolds as if from blue,
But how it feels forgetting things in haste,
In embracing sorrows knocking on door,
Feeling full, times be prime, or not in rhyme,
In giving to life more than one may get—
    Ah, like a child building castles in joy:
    Happy to build, happy should tides destroy!

The best seller, How of Happiness, says: 50% of happiness is determined by genes (nature)— likes-dislikes, cravings of senses. Ten percent comes from experiences of life as such, while 40% of happiness depends upon how man responds to these circumstances— what he makes of what he gets. In other words half of happiness is ruled by birth, and the rest by life— how it is lived, how he responds to life that unfolds. At least 40% of happiness is in man's hands.

Of course likes and dislikes, governed by senses, also can be changed. And hence most of it is made in mind. This is what the poem-ending couplet avers. The first six lines rhyme seriatim with the next six.

- Sonnets | 11.06.13 |

48

A brick of guilt

Fair wisdom there's in keeping my mouth shut,
Believes so amid three one mouth discreet,
Let me not my digits on my own cut,
I know, the axe when falls, falls on my feet.

The second fumes within, silent he burns,
And blurts out words vain in impotent rage,
The rope when tightens still, he turtle turns,
Values in life look fine if free from wage.

World has e'er been like this, believes the third,
Crows all come black, what use boiling my blood?
And trickles grow when forging furious flood,
The how and why of values get nigh blurred.

The burial vault our own is when on built,
We, blissful blind, donate a brick of guilt.

This is an impotent little cry on what has been happening in the country today. For, we can blame none but ourselves. After all, we get only what we deserve.

- Sonnets | 04.07.13 |

Good things are good for their brief date

Heady earth-scent1 hugging droplets of rain—
A gift but of first spell and gone ere long,
A fragrance scarce repeated soon again,
For, short and sweet does come a pleasant song.
A rare delight 'tis walking thro the field
Of bluebells in late April, amid spring
In blossom, casting a brief spell, soon killed;
So short be the cherry blossom's inning,
So fragile be her bloom, so delicate,
A light spring rain can cause petals to fall;
Perhaps, good things are good for their brief date,
Take life's transience, honeymoon's brief call.
      Yea, all things lovely in life short-lived are,
      No wonder, beauty nor youth stretches far.

---

1. The monsoon fragrance has a name: petrichor, from Greek petra= stone, ichor= fluid that flows in veins of gods. This fragrance comes when the oil exuded by certain plants (absorbed in dry season by clay-based soils) is released into air along with geosmin, a by-product of bacteria. The whole complex phenomenon produces a subtle heady smell.

But I must confess, after knowing the science behind this fine art of the first-rain-kissed earth, the fragrance seems not as heady as it used to be in all my innocent years ere!

- Sonnets | 05.07.13 |

The fragrance of memories

Capturing cakes' cologne, smell of sea-shores,
Who would, I wonder, such weird things want?
Fair 'tis if memory stores and restores,
Isn't better still to wipe cobwebs that haunt?
Man may be charmed by a caressing smell,
A stray gem, jewel, may well a man move,
But a set of them would sure steal a spell,
So is body bouquet of lady love.
Imagine scents of life tied down to chain—
The fragrant feel of a first-born in arm,
Her awe inspiring purity so warm,
Delicate scent of earth fetched on first rain.
    Science may such a prison make per chance,
    Can it e'er cap old memory's fragrance?

Researchers seem to have invented a camera that can record smells, and can 'see' the old memory in photograph, and smell the-then prevailing scents too! A funnel sucks in the smell's particles, and deposits them in a polymer preparing a graph so that the same fragrance, say, of a birthday cake, can be released and re-experienced.

This piece however throws in a poetic caveat. Some agonies of life are best forgotten and buried. Some still have their charm in recalling, ever so vaguely, reaching into the cupboard of life that was, rummaging for a fragment there, a remnant here in 'remembrance of things past'— the kind of memories, when taken a whole, some hurting, some comforting, which no camera can truly capture, save the mind's.

- Sonnets (Happenings) | 06.07.13 |

Man cannot the big picture see

Some[1] say that Fate punishes men for sins,
For misdeeds, as a mother would her child;
Some[2] say, 'tis laws of karma ever since;
Yet others[3]: good and bad bare views are wild,
Evil's unreal; and grace personified,
God 'lone has means to view the whole scene well,
And man of meagre means aught feel deprived,
A blind can scarce a whole elephant spell.

Perchance, evil nor He's no-matter good,
Nor may man be a fair creation— His,
Goodness grows rising above Maya's hood,
As He is, man is Truth Awareness, Bliss[4].
    To me the world evil, good nor is bad,
    And no man joyous be if never sad.

---

1. This is as per Old Testament. The acts of God are seen to be just, didactic, and oft penal.
2. Every action, good or bad, has a reaction and fetches fruits, that man must enjoy or suffer as per Karmic Laws, an Indic thought.
3. This is known as Leibnitz view.
4. Vedantic view. Man is the mirror image of God, Brahman, and is sat-chit-ananda: Existence-Consciousness-Bliss. Man is therefore essentially good, without evil. The good and evil that we see as duals are creations of Maya, illusion. Events in the world are God's lila, or play that we see with the eyes of Maya.

But without going into this heady intellectualism, this sonnet tries to give an uncomplicated view of heart.

- Sonnets | 07.07.13 |

One truth, apart we see

If I things one way see
And you apart from me,
I see that as fruit's rind
Which, when ripens gets red—
Of degree, not of kind,
Openness lies in head,
Look at red and violet—
Poles apart, one spectrum,
Both dance one tune to hum,
Make light white, white can get.
Plain truths seem hard to see,
Take waves, water in sea,
        In moonless night so dark,
        See dogs at one thing bark.

- Sonnets | 06.08.13 |

To raise a child

We spend wide-eyed years of a child
Chastising how to walk, to talk,
And thence many his tender year
Be-warning: stay near, nice and dear,
Not letting him to wow his walk,
Not this, nor that, ne'er to be wild;
And so busy are we to preach
By dictates of a spoken word,
That we all but forget to teach
By acts of self, not words so blurred,
Ensuring scarce he walks his talk,
Nor walking a self-trodden walk!
    We marvel still poet as can:
    That child is the father of man!

- Sonnets | 07.08.13 |

The world unwilling to wake

In a fond dream seems this world caught
As if a sprawling place in fire,
An inferno, huge burning pyre;
If saved from this hellhole blaze not,
It'd get burnt to ashes like reed.
Yet, indifferent in this world,
One end burns, the rest takes no heed,
Oblivious, at peace, blissful, lulled!
Minuscule few can see things well,
Wide eyed, unable to react,
Proverbial frog as if in spell;
And whoso came wanting to act,
> *Paid a price with self at the stake,*
> *In waking what wished not to wake!*

- Sonnets | 08.08.13 |

True wealth— wonders of world

Long shut, opened I have my blinkered eyes,
He you thought poor, Ritchie rich do I find,
And found me poorer but a wee-bit wise,
A heritage rich from the farm I've mined:
Wealth too weak is to help make one happy.
We've but one dog, that boy has many more,
Our swimming pool far too small seems to me,
The streams the boy bathes in for long miles roar,
Our lamp in garden— you think brightest is,
Bare if its light burns bright beyond terrace,
While million stars splendour that boy to please,
And endless open skies in sleep him grace.
    One watching wonders of world thence is rich,
    Poor is him, left mundane riches to reach.

A rich father once takes his son to see poverty of the world so that he realises how truly rich and fortunate they were. They went to a nearby village, lived in small hut of a poor boy, ate dry bread without butter, and slept under open skies. On returning home next day, the father asked an obvious question, but his son had a surprise in store for him.

- Sonnets | 09.08.13 |

When God created man

Let there limit none to man's wisdom be,
God thought, working a lump of clay, did pause
Reflecting still, a wise one that he was,
Let's see what he does with stupidity!
Many may feel now: well, that was not fair,
But I'd rather it was His foresight rare;
With wisdom man would just so much height rise
As his idiocy would nigh let him reach,
Yet, seldom high enough to realise,
Wither goes he— devil, deep sea, or ditch!
His wisdom vouchsafing way otherwise,
Inanity his rising to heights rare,
Promising him an impossible prize,
And lo, God has no more patience to spare!

- Sonnets | 12.08.13 |

The paradox: purse and appetite

As a poet, perhaps grey like me, said
Thinking of youth: 'We pine for all things good,
Our oldest thoughts . . . dwell on forbidden food',
And joy is maid of no modest maw made.

And passion for food fails to dissipate,
A river in spate sourced from modest means,
Enduring if on no discretion leans,
But world on extreme has erred, love or hate.

And as seductive spells food, in extremes,
Eve happy was not— Just one apple bite?
Bellies may belong to bread, brain to creams,
The twain together makes good appetite.

Pity, youth has keen maw— no money's might,
Yet, age means has, nor hunger for a bite!

- Sonnets (humour) | 04.09.13 |

Life is a waiting room

Mother's womb, a prison term of slow gears,
Soul must wait to be delivered, in tears,
And waiting game ne'er seems to end— old grime:
Tall tomes of learning, tests and testing time,
College and career, cutting edge of knife,
Grub for the goose and gander, goodly life,
Profession and promotions and progress,
Waiting in winding queues whence end the faith,
Till tired, awaiting freedom from this mess;
And when all waiting makes one far too old,
To wait first for hereafter on the hold,
Diseased, disillusioned, at last for death!
    Laud nor applaud, the game ends not as yet,
    Sent back, the waiting cycles renewed get!

What's life? There are as many answers as are people. This poem says, 'Life is a waiting room'. Man waits all life for something or the other, and dies disillusioned, his train called desire not arriving still.

- Sonnets | 08.09.13 |

Faith

Silent does sleep supine time, hard to wake,
Coil unto endless coil, face on the hide,
The world unfolds whilst unperturbed beside,
Yet, faith in an unborn womb seems awake.
A common link links— each a serene lake,
While eternity in its bosom holds,
Faith moves on gathering moss as unfolds,
Death, nor devastation, can ever shake
It in its onward march for fair or worse,
Whilst nations get effaced a whole from earth,
Whilst kings and mighty kingdoms lose their worth,
Soiled whilst flow holy waters of rivers,
 Whilst supine time watches helpless like ghost,
 Divine faith anchors reaching safer coast.

- Sonnets | 01.10.13 |

O Make room for joy

'Seeds of setbacks when grow— you to destroy,
'Make room enough for every joy to groom,
'Spare a li'le niche for every heart-felt buoy,
'And see that joys grow free, gloom has no room',
A voice said, 'make it with love, not somehow';
And yet we feel every inch is crowded
With things one day we loved— but no more now;
'Clear all clutters crowding the room', it said:
'Let no moments buried be in busy-ness,
'Have a date with your soul, with solitude,
'Clear resentments poaching on precious space,
'Neutralise acidic bitter, feel good,
Yet, came worries, claimed tenancy, old dame,
And joys failed to fill up with honest claim.

- Sonnets (humour) | 04.11.13 |

Who are you?

Flesh, blood, mind, nor whatso be in brain lined,
Nor whatso I know nor ever ego,
Nor yet five senses can make what 'I' is,
Nor is made of five elements as said—
Ether nor space, water nor ever earth,
Nor fire nor air, nor am I known by birth,
I've father nor ever have I mother,
Nor do I have friends nor foes nor brother,
I have a name given to me as came,
By any a name still I'm all the same,
Ye ask, 'pray who art thou? What should I say?
The only thing I can say: what I'm not;
   Eternal joy and bliss, all of knowing,
   Unending love, I'm what makes conscious thing!

His guru Govindapada once asked **shankarāchārya** 'who are you?' He, a little boy of barely eight years at that time, answered in Sanskrit verse known as **ātma-shaṭakaṁ** or **nirvāṇa-shaṭakaṁ** which has a refrain: **shivohaṁ shivohaṁ**. This Sonnet based on the verse, but no translation, has most of its lines with internal rhyme save a few.

- Sonnets | 07.11.13 |

Time 'tis for me to go

In your house garden did I live long,
Saying, time there's for all things to go,
All along chirping, chanting my song . . .

I liked greens of gardens, nothing wrong,
The fragrance of flowers, of things grow,
Nothing wrong if I liked my own song.

Winds of change then charmed things all along,
Telling all, it's time to make a mo,
In yours I made my house O for long.

I now sing last few lines of my song,
No one is above change, aught I go,
Because, comes to an end every song.

Life's naught but endless change, nothing wrong,
Let me not overstay welcome, so,
Time has come to go singing my song.

You won't sure remember me for long—
None does in this world of right with wrong—
That in house of yours I lived so long,
O chirping and chanting same old song.

The common house sparrow seems on the way out in most of India. This
is what it might have said in her last passing song, set in anapaest metre.

- Villanelles | 02.12 13 |

The truth of thine beauty

In this make-believe world of illusion,
The beauty of thine absolute may seem
To me, in this time and space of heaven,
Reality as seen still is no dream.
Truth they say's truth only if seamless whole,
May be; but thine beauty's truth never dies
If frozen, chopped to bits, or sent to coal,
For, parts transcending when to truth must rise.
You and I, my love, live in a rare world
Wherein the holder, beholder beside
Of beauty, both the self-same be a bird,
And in the same time and space do reside.
    Now, if both of these birds do e'er exist,
    The scenery and seer, me god, same beast!

Most men oft face this situation when their love objects ask them about their beauty. And for answer they have to resort to some vague abra cadabra, as in this piece.

- Sonnets (humour) | 03.12.13 |

Broom, our hope

I

Things that should be show-cased we tend to hide;
'Pon a tallest pedestal we oft place
Things that stink even as our bloated pride,
No wonder they cry for fair open space.

Yet, a poor man no such dilemma has,
Show-case has he, nor e'er any a case,
Pedestal nor carpet; may God him bless,
He always has broom, a thing of bare base.

Brooms many a use have, many a face,
Rich or poor, king, commons, it's always there,
Ahead, behind, in the end wins the race,
For ages this has not changed a whit bare;
    And one last thing, ah, we still have in hand,
    Hope, things at last are on a turning bend.

II

The hand and its ilk in years have done little,
Slogans, postures, and little more than words,
The pot besides blames of dark deeds poor kettle,
People grin and bear, 'sure we're helpless herds!'

But those that take to brooms work with bare hands,
Blame nor yet back-pat, nor be tongue their act,
And we hope be the morrow's setting trends,
To whom precede acts a matter of fact.

'But you can scarce use brooms in dirty pond',
Protests an old grower of lotus there,
Yet lotus cleansed nor pledged, redeemed no bond,
The pond remaining murky ever ere!
    Beware still; brooms oft sweep under carpet,
    Beware of them; make none a beloved pet.

The poem obviously alludes to the forthcoming elections and dirty one-upmanship. All existing players proving no good, people placed their bets on a new front, which too (as the later events showed) proved no good. And the loud-mouth lotus won. True, in politics nothing sticks. Lotus or no, they are all non-stick! This twain of a sonnet warned in vain.

- Sonnets, (happenings) | 04.12.13 |

I remember

Her smile a beacon of grace,
And her visage of warm face
Hinted, she with her heart was home,
The way she made me feel at home
Under her sprawling large dome
Made of love, whenso I went in.
I'd feel as if in warm sunshine
If weather was or not so fine—
And was welcome so well within
With a smile fresh as sunrise,
Dawn was or dusk the day when dies,
Rare was smile not smiling with eyes!
    Yet, weather changes, warning there's none,
    What made her change, who knows but heaven!

- Sonnets | 02.01.12 |

Let bad banished be by better

Books banned banished not be nor burnt to naught,
Nor thoughts nor ideas be confined to jail,
No censored art does stay for long unsought,
As all inquests condemned are to derail;
Societies if they be left free to fail,
At times tense in dissent and friction-prone,
Like turbulent ocean be-caught on gale,
Be proof: freedom breathes big on its own.

No art obscene be, book nor painting drawn,
For, all obscenity like beauty lies
In beholder's eye that sees what's ere sown,
As most minds scarce from their base level rise,
    It's hard indeed better bailiff to see
    For bad idea than one that better be.

Much of intolerance seen in India today seems stage-managed and promoted to win votes. Take the ban on Salman Rushdie on attending a Lit Fest in Jaipur. Take court cases on well-known painter M F Hussein, who had to stay away from his country of birth till he died in London; take Taslima Nasreen of Bangladesh being driven out of West Bengal; take banning of books, paintings, and movies, even historical essays. But have they remained banned? What is banned seldom becomes banal. If anything books banned become better known, if not best sellers. The way out is indicated in the couplet concluding this Sonnet.

- Sonnets | 08.01.12 |

Father of man a child is not

Early we err, a child's when not yet three,
Soon as in wonder he begins to think,
By hammering his head with thoughts scarce free,
School of heft than height happens him to sink;
Society then conspires to take over,
Leaving him 'lone not for a lone minute,
Building a boundary, rules binding to shore,
Ties, tethers that lay strangling a limit;
Soon comes spouse and children—what misfortune!
To hoist him a hostage, a hackney horse,
Mere sight of risk digs him deep into dune,
Poor him, done and dusted ere running course!

And whoso said, 'He that holds a child's soul
Holds whole nation', a square seems in round hole!

- Sonnets | 09.01.12 |

To see mother masking as Maya

She gave more and more toys to her cry-child,
And yet, without a look he wailed more still,
Growing restless, disconsolate and wild,
And mother as she was knew what was ill;
So is Maya the Mother of us all,
Piling in our path a pageant of toys,
That we learn wise to be, virtuous tall,
That we ferret out pain faking as joys;
Mother's love clad in illusion we see,
The light transcending darkness, truth entwined
In clouds of ignorance, water of sea
Veiling as waves, to see glue that does bind
  Us; 'tis on reaching top of tallest roof
  That we know, one it is with floor— for proof!

- Sonnets | 10.01.12 |

Seeking depth, not ocean

Child she is of heights, cradled by the crest
Of a mountain, born a tiny bare brook,
Dancing down sprightly at life's spring, modest
Still hiding oft in hillocks, cranny's nook,
In no time to resurface once again,
In new avatar, a wide-mouth waterfall,
Cascading down ah in utter disdain,
Meandering river to be in thrall,
And at long last to be an estuary,
Sprawling, shallow, wider and slower still,
Destined to embrace sea, fulfilled to be—
One, with option nor yet a free self-will!
*   Maid, keen to meet her love, nor poetry,*
*   Fluid just flows free forced by gravity.*

Rivers are painted in fancy by poets. Most common being a bride rushing sprightly down to meet her beau, the sea. No one falls for the plain truth: water flows down seeking gravity.

- Sonnets | 03.02.12 |

Death, tail-wind of change

Death! Thou alone maketh man what he's now,
For, when life seeks to take a renewed lease,
It's no end, so, a brief interlude art thou,
Dost thou not bestow balmy life new breeze?
Tail-wind of change, art no punishing rod:
Blowing up stars, turning them angry red,
Pounding tall peaks, protecting else like pod,
Making kings commoners, winners wilted.

It's fine pen-painting life in present tense,
But doubtful putting thee in perfect past;
Let me call thee 'future-in-past' now hence,
To op up past tinged with infinite vast,
    Without thee how'd life see full rainbow range?
    Move on Death, thou art blessing, no revenge.

- Sonnets | 01.09.12 |

Prose and poetry

I wonder why cavemen chose to sing,
Ere using speech communicating,
Perhaps dull prose limits, posits, pretends,
May be to narrow mundane meaning binds,
Or fails to touch heart's deepest core,
Soft frost snow as if blocking freedom's shore,
Or fails to let explore new crests, and finds
No rainbow shades, oft facing dead ends,
And why today's time-starved world speaks,
Perhaps prose touches base heeded by head,
Whilst verses reach rarefied peaks
In far fewer steps if by heart heeded,
And head prefers opting for prose,
A rose as if forgets it's rose.

This sonnet in a mix of tetra and penta-metre has its octave rhymed abccbadd, and the sestet efefgg.

- Sonnets | 05.09.12 |

This world of spectators

Far few actors, spectators so many,
Least living life than watching the world live—
Rudderless in a ship, oar-less at sea,
On rented joy, gathering more than give;
A few playing, a million minds peeping,
A rare few living, all else avoiding,
Cheering like court jesters as if to king!
How can life lived on couch joy ever bring?

A life that does not else than watching scene,
Shrinking in stature, life of spectator—
A spectral shadow staring at square screen,
He that begs joys from a joy-creator,
*   In hope thankless yet this poem I pen,*
*   A voice in wilderness and one in ten!*

- Sonnets | 09.09.12 |

We and all else

Countless creatures repair back to Death's door
Day to day, yet those alive seems to feign,
Oh well, we hail from heaven's deathless shore;
What can be stranger than this, what more vain?
This has been so for ages and still ere,
And shall survive still for long heretofore—
This gulf of 'we and them', that 'we are rare'—
Yet, Time is here everything to devour.

'We' shall rise high 'pon angel's soaring wings,
And all else, hell-bound, shall grow horns on head,
The ill within me scarce to my core clings,
Whilst alien's smallest sin grows gruesome red.
*   We and them might sons be of the same sun,*
*   Yet, they'd suffer hell, and we high heaven!*

- Sonnets | 03.10.12 |

Not life, death is real

I wake one day only for long to sleep,
Suffer my fate to find if life is fake,
And learn not still: what we sow may not reap.

Death is real all through life to creep
In, crawl along like a slithering snake,
I wake one day only for more to sleep.

A friend may not keen friendship keep,
Good death, friendship nor date does break,
And lets me learn: to sow's not soon to reap.

Life is a tiny blip of time, no leap,
To break bread with journeymen, friends to make,
I wake one day only for long to sleep.

To live, forget— not to find meaning deep,
To swim and sink in life's shallow a lake,
'Tis to learn still: to sow is not to reap.

We live and gather light every round trip,
Not life still, death has deeper stake;
I wake one day only for long to sleep,
To try and learn: what we sow may not reap.

- Villanelles | 05.10.12 |

The mystery of 'here' and 'now'

Let people dwell in hist'ry as much can,
Let them love time-stealers called 'was' and 'will',
He that loves here and now is happy man.

Both absurd be, both flightless and as vain,
Buried deep in vales, or unseen beyond hill,
Let people dwell in hist'ry as much can.

If what goes never does return again,
And fleeting moments' all one may have, still,
He that loves here and now is happy man.

The story of man e'er since Time began,
If were to fall in same trap, same evil,
What use dwelling in hist'ry much one can?

Naught whatso changes more relentless than
This twain of time-wasters of wanton will,
He that loves here and now is happy man.

As past pans out on how we choose to pan,
And morrows melt to nought in frozen chill,
Let whoso dwell in hist'ry as much can,
He that loves here and now is happy man.

- Villanelle | 06.10.12 |

Desire

Beginning small, becoming a big beast,
She spurs like cats but speaks nor is she schooled,
A sovereign queen at her life-long feast;
And Muse of every man by her befooled,
Harmless kitten nudging him with soft paw,
Pestering to pay heed, caressing crease,
And much ere he knows she's a raving maw,
If starved, a forest fire on wings of breeze.

Long hath man mused: to be or not to be,
World's Oliver Twist wanting ever more,
And having had the wish seldom happy
Still; hard it is showing desire the door—
*   For, men dream of champagne and caviar,*
*   When all they deserve is hot dogs and beer.*

- Sonnets | 02.11.12 |

Heal thyself, or else

I

Two scores of ripe years ere, remember I,
At shower, shaving mirror, soothing hair,
Bending elbow when turned annoying nigh,
I wonder when, how my hurt walked in there
Unknown to me, as seasons oft set in
Before we know, till one day forced are we
To tune into the change though never keen;
But more than pain, the ailment annoyed me.

For, the medic I met, cool as was I,
Tad too sure called it a tennis elbow,
Protested I not having played the game,

Muffling a suppressed laugh respectfully,
The doc unmoved as e'er let me this know:
Nailed by any a name it'd pain the same.

II

And prescribed a pain pacifying drug,
Me not a kind to treat pointers of pain,
Rooted in the cause of root cause, I shrugged,
The pain, not being un-seasonal rain,
Persisted, gaining slow intensity,
The devil in doc now vindicated,
Looking kind, stern-eyed still, nodded at me,
Counsel my own had left me defeated!

O'er-ruled, a rebel on knees, out elbowed,
Bowed to submission, folding my left sleeve,
I looked as if explanation was owed,

He looked up then a stern verdict to give:
There's no escape seeds are once duly sowed,
Ailments you scarce from solar space receive.

III

In was called nursing help, and like a cow
Was led to slaughter house, I all but thought,
The wise me cursing the rebel me now,
And I followed— in worse of worries wrought;
Thinking of thermal waves— for half an hour
A day; relief if there be it could worse
Be than the pain, headache long to hover,
I learn with it to live —in quiet curse.

And when they thought of changing course, it's time
For what if: like tides wisdoms wane or wax,
But docs have reasons if or not in rhyme,

'I need take a goodly look at your X-
Ray'; eyed my arm, poor thing was caught in crime,
And did look like a bleeding knife or axe.

IV

'Malign growth, there's no sign', the doc declared
Swirling into the scene I waited in,
With enough hints, his wisdom as he aired,
As if a kindly heart heaved in within,
His dire demeanours still notwithstanding;
'And yet', added, looks darkening somewhat,

'See on the left some growth—in a soft ring,
'I've reasons to suspect and doubt than naught'.

I see not else than my upper-arm bone,
Humerus as is called, but I'd like to
Call it funny, fun having too far gone!

But felt, silence may seem a good virtue
To one on wrong side of a stick or stone;
I weighed in his weighty words of sharp hue.

V

'Need a few more searching tests to be sure,
'But what we see seems serious enough still',
What else, grin or grimace I aught endure,
Yet unsure quite what a greater evil
Was: ailment or treatment of my elbow!
A vision of an endless dark tunnel
Flashed in mind that dark was and no less dull,
Something beyond the pain churned in my maw.

'Take a course of killer tabs to start with,
'Your elbow should be under careful eyes',
He said, looking at my bone like hound-smith.

But as if pregnant the swelling did rise,
A cyst in unknown liquid— my close kith,
Guesses galore and a gag of surmise!

VI

'We'll aspirate the liquid', he thence said,
'If liquid goes, I hope the swelling too';
My arm dulled he worked— large needle in aid,

And felt as if Everest looked dwarf in view.
A few days and liquid returned to base,
Returned the swelling too as it ere was,
Respite from pain, nor from hospital chase,
And wondered karmas caught up with my cause.

All through, pain but a minor irritant
Was, and lived normal life as did before,
If only avoided I had it all.

And what with all docs and drugs, my tenant
In elbow cosy did well stay indoor—
In comfy little cyst, safe in soft wall!

VII

My Healer, looking graver than e'er ere,
His cocky flair deserting never once,
Swirled his chair round— across glass pane to stare,
As if to get inspired by Providence;
More dumb than mute I curse my accursed fate.
'Feel happy it's only left hand',
He declared, mouth open an ajar gate,
'In worst case will amputate if can't mend'!

'Irritating, and though it does take long,
'Tuber is always easy to get cured—
'Soft type or bone, cancer I hope not is'.

He tuned it out as if a movie song,
And assuming that I was well assured,
There came the costs, ah with consummate ease.

VIII

Getting none his wisdom home and fair,
Pleading as though guilty and penitent,
I whose dream had turned to nightmare,
When pressed to know— doctor to patient,
'A graveyard let's say, infection on run,
'A cyst enveloping much like a fort,
'But look at Nature's marvellous li'le action—
'A compromise settlement out-of-court'!

To cut it short, pain visiting again,
The cyst was cut asunder to the roots,
And yet, the tests when came, came with no clue.

Not in vain still, gone was persisting pain,
Gone was the cause, me left with bitter fruits—
A safeguard root treatment— tabs and pricks due!

IX

I oft feel if he that treated me knew
The mystery that human body is,
That it takes two hundred muscles, not few,
To take but one baby step with some ease;
That, body's veins when stretched end to end nigh,
A pair of belts round earth's bosom is made;
That, cells in a myriad of deluge when die,
An equal sum in even time gets bred.

But nigh li'le is known of the universe
That lies within— much as we outer space,
Our grasp on ailing body is still worse;

There's as much darkness as there's light apace.
Socrates knew, 'he lone hath thinking mind
That knows: knowledge known shall e'er lag behind'.

And so, if we should let sleeping dogs lie,
Should we not let bodies heal—of drugs dry?

This is a sequence of nine sonnets. The last line of the preceding sonnet is not the first line of the next sonnet; nor is the first line of the first sonnet, the last line of the last sonnet as is often the case. The last sonnet has an extra couplet.

- Sonnets | 03.11.12 |

Fourteen beautiful birds on wings

A baker as packs thirteen eggs to claim
A good dozen, a sonneteer— fourteen
Sweet lines in praise of poem's slender frame,
That her mysterious marvels ever green
Remain; yet wants his fledglings to well hatch
O gorgeous birds to be, ready to fly
In time together in one single batch,
Or in formations that such species try.

The eight of them in front to face all strife,
The six that trail, as if in counterpoint,
Resolve to soothe— ah, sonnet's very life,
As Volta, some poets choose to anoint,
    And the last two, twain wings of a couplet,
    Come with a short song ending the nugget.

- Sonnets | 04.11.12 |

Sonnets: brevity binds

Some worshipped when guineas and gold heirloom
That lay buried all year in vaults and cells,
The young when fire crackers, old fret from room,
In temples beat when drums, cymbals and bells,
Time 'tis when to invoke Goddess of wealth
On thirteenth day of crescent waning moon,
Worried of smoke, noise, of my shying health,
And lost in thoughts of my life's raging noon,
Amid festive spirit, what with loud boom
Around, it was hard to constrain my mood
In the confines of constricting small room,
And made me on sonnet's sparse plots to brood—
How brevity binds straying pens from drift,
How compact frames poet's spirit uplift!

- Sonnets | 07.11.12 |

In memory of my Monk Hills

Dear Monk hills, your lessons rest etched in head,
What books taught like childhood has been dead past,
How memories— happy and not still last
Many a long decade though left unread
For years, e'er since I roamed your breasts, brown beds
In search of sweet treats in your shades serene;
So deep an impress easy never fades
From any a mind's wistful eyes, so keen
For raw adventures and innocent thrills,
In pallid brown, brawny tints of summer
Sun, filtering through grey garments of hills,
Ham-handed pranks and dry girlie humour,
  Derisive of today's balding grave cares,
  In fond hope: how if Time stops, old time spares!

Monk Hills: There were two small hills (*bava no dungar* in local lingo) close to one of my schools. To many they were *timbher* hills for the fruits (lemon sized berries with a hard brown shell when ripe, containing whitish sweet pulp), which grew wild aplenty. The 'sweet treats' refers to these fruits.

- Sonnets | 01.12.12 |

Mutating morals

The morals in men once we much admired—
A kindly heart ensconced in unkind age,
Generous, and way far this worldly wired,
Honest and open like a printed page,
Empathy, understanding, feeling heart
That beats for all, and simple nor yet sure,
Free from a smart aleck's much-rehearsed art—
The tribe has lost today old-worldly lure.

And those that we did readily detest—
A cutting sharp head like a two-edged sword,
Meanest of mind wrapped in self-interest,
And greed to grab and gather piles to hoard,
    O seem to turn today's triumphant page
    Of best-seller a book that spells image.

- Sonnets | 01.01.11 |

Thank hell that heaven's sweet

Loveliness of lotus from dirt doth rise,
From scorching heat come cool showers as rain,
And every joy doth spring from pits of pain,
So seem sorrows sent to us O to size.
There's charm, nor venture in life sans challenge,
If road ahead is straight and smoother laid,
If life always shines bright hues of orange,
Bewitching if comes every teen-age maid;
If life lingers, a bed of roses quite,
Roses, thorns duly condemned to exile,
Life whose black be banished, life always bright,
All pleasure-no pain does make it sterile.
    Crib not O Mind problems may keep a cropping,
    Thank, troubles come and whet dull will from rusting.

- Sonnets | 07.04.11 |

Whatso might happen happens still

Gods if churned oceans of vast wisdom
To get venom, get nectar of life,
Whipping when venomous a life's strife,
Man may get crown of thorn with kingdom.

And who ever ask cocks crowing shrill,
If it's time for the sun to arise,
The sun shall— and shine a scorching noon,
And would fall to depths till midnight's moon,
Sure to rise again as dark night dies,
And the new dawn when as always dawns,
It rises to set that no one mourns;
For, what might well happen, happens still.

And thing that comes to be comes and dies,
As venom-nectar's one for the wise.

With atypical rhyme scheme, this sonnet is set in anapaest metre, three feet.

- Sonnets | 08.04.11 |

The scare-crow and avian friends

Me friendless lone, what will I say to crowd?
What with voice suppressed, muted, bent and bowed,
Doing a job that makes me, none else proud—
To scare my friends from this sowed field ere ploughed.
The scare-crow stood open mouth, not allowed
To open up his heart, but feeling proud,
Worried of brother birds, the avian crowd,
The skies o'er head with not a single cloud,
Oh hungry mouths around and me unmoved,
With all dead who shall I scare with this shroud?
Me, in this grey field with so much hope sowed,
Me, mute and all else O crying aloud!

O there, just do your job; make yourself proud,
Someone's doing His— worry for the crowd.

___

This little scare-crow is split apart on the call of duty on one hand, and heart-felt concern about his winged friends, against whose interest he has to work. He is worried about clear, cloudless skies. If it no more rains, what would his friends do? With no crop, what will he guard, and against whom? He is lost amid these sentiments, and a voice comes from afar, telling him, his duty it is to do his job, never to worry about the outcome. For, there is someone else who has volunteered to worry. The scare crow's single-minded worry about his avian friends is expressed here with all the fourteen lines taking but a single rhyme.

___

- Sonnets | 09.04.11 |

When heart conspires with head

Poet whose head heeds to no rigid rules,
Who walks tall warded off by a stiff cane,
A penchant pen in pocket, walking sane,
Heart singing harvest songs learnt at no schools;
For, art by nature is no child of brain,
As swimmers sought are from no shallow pools,
One, wanderlust seldom in parkways cools,
Nor a fertile pen goes dry should ink drain.

How does a wild flower her fragrance spread?
The blossom on stray leas still has fond friend,
Far from a plucking up and prying hand;
Freedom unfelt poetic heart keeps red,
Less relied be when rules rich spectrum land,
To fertile pens, when heart conspires with head.

- Sonnets | 04.07.11 |

In a beauteous monsoon eve

A beauteous monsoon eve, calm as deep sea,
Holy hours standing still but for slow rain,
The setting sun breathless, tired, somewhat sane,
Seeming to sink unto serenity,
Whilst grey clouds in triumph gliding with glee,
Unmindful of the serene prayer time,
The song of rain well with the hour when rhyme,
Something connects me with tranquillity;
Monsoon summons when solemnest of thoughts,
The dying sun of evening looks divine
When seasons merge seamless with passing year,
Month by month, day by day, like tiny dots,
Man tires not admiring Nature's design—
In faith or fear or love, far from me clear!

- Sonnets | 06.07.11 |

The spring ardent does call

The shocking news, like weight of a dead stone,
When fell upon my worried weary breast,
My mind, half anticipating the phone
And cruel blow, my head suffered modest;
But my worries were for unknown morrows—
How to mute memories once and for all,
Turn off traumatised soul's steely woes,
For one aught learn to live, arise from pall;

For, spring ardent does call, so do the birds,
There lives a festival of life around,
As I know time, nor tide waits for kind words,
This life's dramas by fate released astound.
  Earth for all worth is scarce the sole's sole sphere,
  For, life behind curtains too happens here.

- Sonnets | 13.07.11 |

All nature seems to while time and wait

All Nature seems to wait with steely will—
The slow sloth and snails scarce feel frowned by time,
Bears in bliss hibernate with willing will,
'O let it be, wait' seems their panache prime.
A wet day awaits sun, springs wintry chill,
So do doldrums of June; patience no crime!
And winter weathers till melts frozen snow,
Dreaming no idle dreams of spring-warmed wood,
Trees stand still, meditate an inch to grow
In all year to fetch fruits of fortitude;
But bees seem all astir, honey to bring,
And birds on busy wings build nests, singing.
    Sure, Nature has her reason; man weary
    Of serene state, aught for rat race hurry.

- Sonnets | 14.07.11 |

Joy is the way

Slow and serene when I walked at the jheel[1],
Wearing on my visage a pleasant smile,
Relaxed to core and deep-set ease to feel,
All weary thoughts I left behind a mile.
The seed of joy and bliss, of peace and love,
I scarce knew a perennial source in me,
Was hampered, cramped— me always on the move,
That blue skies moved me not, nor depth of sea,
Nor walking leisured walk, I chose to run
For vaguest reason, when a peaceful pause
Would have put me in touch with my soul's heaven,
Such was the lure of chasing that ne'er was.
    Too bad I realise this, this late day,
    That there's no way to joy, joy is the way[2].

---

1. jheel: Hindi, for a shallow, sprawling lake.
2. There is no way to peace, peace is the way. - M Gandhi

- Sonnets | 05.08.11 |

The march of time

The New Year dawns, hope and half wish,
Old when seems to fade lost of dream,
And March marches, chill left behind,
In April spring springs forth full brim,
May-June then sizzle in hot noon,
Mercury up like pressured steam,
Monsoon turns all grey into green,
Rivers and lakes flowing full rim;
Autumn and fall take o'er in turn,
Reminding of impending grim
Of chill-frost 'gain in endless chain;
All Nature's mortal born as seem;
 Spirit only chases lost dreams,
  Nature when gives up— or so deems.

The lines with odd numbers run rhyme-less, while all even ones share one single rhyme throughout.

- Sonnets | 08.08.11 |

My thoughts go to fruits still

Some trees fail to flower ere seasons wear,
Or with unequal sun comes when the season,
Or flowers when find no love fruits to bear;
Yet, cool inviting shelter from the sun,
It's leafs, more than flowers and fruits, me beckon;
So seems the life designed well by the heaven,
So knowing when I try to live my life,
Oft fruitless, and as often fruity rife,
Yet, wonder why thoughts oft stick to no roots—
And thinking of spring-flowers home to bring,
In life's late eve when harvest songs I sing—
That some fateful flowers might bring me fruits!
    Ere, Adam was warned of forbidden fruit,
    We know how destiny played tempting lute.

- Sonnets | 01.09.11 |

O to live and let go

If what I call an end beginning is,
New destiny when beckons, life past lull,
And every beginning an end— to seize—
An end, a short breath and an interval—
Cosmic design when renders a new art,
Decides to rekindle the old spirit,
That each beginning gets a balmy start,
And journey old with path anew is lit.

If only I learn to live and let go,
And be in tune with Nature, not a beast
In fight nor fright nor flight— that does well know,
O to flow with the flow ne'er to resist.
     Caterpillar does call its end no death,
     And basks as butterfly—new birth new faith.

Sonnets often get born on the cusp of unresolved dilemma, as this one was. Here, after an introduction all the eight lines speak as if in one breath, and there comes the dilemma, 'If only I learn to live and let go'. The sonnet ends with a philosophical thought, a couplet, still unresolved.

- Sonnets | 02.09.11 |

O Singer of the epic war history

O Singer of epic war history,
Of brazen battlefields, long desolate,
O Singer of life, liberties hoary,
Bhagavad-Gita is thine ageless glory.

Outlived hast this song an endless story,
The dead heroes surviving still in state,
Frustrated of ill fate but scarce sorry,
O Singer of epic war history.

Yudhishthir's dharma, Arjun's archery,
Bheeshma's oath, Bheemsen's bravery,
Confined can scarce be to the Pearly Gate,
And sung hast thou Gita's ageless glory.

And ye O bard, two roles in one carry:
Poet laureate, progenitor so great,
O born in a river, mother's ferry,
O Singer of epic war history.

Ye sang thine song in such a swell flurry,
The god of wisdom[1], more than adequate,
Lost in deep thought oft felt weary,
O Singer of ancient ageless glory,

For mortal pens 'pon earth of great worry
It is to try e'en to translate[2],
O Singer of epic war history,
O Singer of ancient ageless glory.

---

1. Vyasa, the creator of Mahabharata approached Ganesha, who could write with great speed, to pen down the epic. He agreed but warned the poet not to make him wait. Vyasa put in a counter condition: Okay, but don't take anything down without understanding it. And so was created an epic of at least hundred thousand verses, or four hundred thousand poetic lines.

2. I have done a poetic translation from the original Sanskrit and I know how formidable a task it is.

This is a Villanelle— a bit way out. The tersest, that normally becomes a quatrain only in the last stanza, becomes so in all. Also, the first and the third lines of the first stanza are repeated with some modifications.

- Villanelle | 02.10.11 |

Death of flirting

No prelude perhaps to lightning affair,
Nor infidel heart's heist to just explore,
Routine good manners, not if eye flutter,
A frisson, thrill— frowned, favoured, or deemed fair;
A harmless celebration of one sex
With the 'ther— a woman well nigh confirming,
She's still female, a male that he's no lax.
I know not what drives dearth of good old flirting.

She has her head to blame, rebel of heart,
Lad-like demeanour called feminism,
That male mystique turns timid, if not tart,
Gallantry's gone, chivalry's frozen firm;
Wake up, Venus, show as ere all thine stars,
Before men migrate to an angry Mars.

It seems in Britain good old art of flirting has gone almost dead. The traditional male etiquette, chivalry, and gallantry survive today only in historical texts, and young man has turned timid to make even an eye contact for the fear of sexual harassment or personal embarrassment. As a result, even a harmless appreciative compliment has dried down. Even in India, the land of nymphs, *apsaras*, *naayikas*, and *dasis*, flirting as a fine art has got all but frozen. And what was not ere long mere dearth of flirting is now a virtual death.

This simple sonnet explores, in a somewhat humorous tone, why. The answer comes in the Volta voicing from the 9th line.

- Sonnets | 06.10.11 |

To love is to give

Burning within, in love for an eon,
The sun ne'er once demanded, nor did fret,
'You owe me lifetime of unredeemed debt';
For, sacrifice is what makes up the sun,
Yet, getting plundered, polluted for long,
She too suffered 'pon bosom every dent,
And mutely winced at every greedy wrong,
True mother, she showed still li'le resentment.

And sun knows: spent up when blow would it lean,
Too faint to light up all the solar skies,
The love that goes to paint the earth bright green,
Shall show grey, and she, bleeding bosom, dies;
She knows: love's not lent to hearts long to stay,
Love is no love until given away[1]!

---

1.   From Oscar Hammerstein, who said,
          Love in your heart wasn't put there to stay—
          Love isn't love till you give it away!

- Sonnets | 07.10.11 |

Twain of paths trodden by men

If there be ways for passing from this world—
One, lit with light o' truth, or else with blight,
Of deeds washed in white light, or in dark night,
By birds of filial feather as I've heard;
He that passeth in light, knoweth his way
To Pearly Gate, eternal light to earn,
The 'ther, lost in labyrinthine alley,
And failing on Judgment Day, aught return.

The Lord doth bear a beacon of bright haze,
And weareth wisp of lustrous-darkling veils,
That no man gets dazed in His radiant gaze,
He showeth light, hailing that no man fails,
That he does find hope in his darkling days,
O to focus on brightest in strange ways.

The first few lines are inspired from Bhagavad-Gita.
See verse # 8.26 that I translate:

This twain of paths trodden here for long,
One bright, other as dark as wrong,
One, to the state of no return doth lead,
To mortal world the other may tread.

Inspiration is also drawn from:

God has 70,000 veils of light and darkness, if He were to remove them, the radiant splendours of His face would burn up whoever was reached by His gaze. – Hadith

Light and darkness are the world's eternal ways.

- Zarathrustra

- Sonnets | 08.10.11 |

In death equal made

The cinders left of Peepal pose no proof
How holy 'pon the earth might be tree's spell,
Nor would dust claim if came from highest roof
Of a hallowed church, or floor ere it fell;
Whether the dust was blown off by tiny
A burst of breeze, or world-wind at full spate;
No keeper can pronounce its pedigree,
No priest can predicate its sublime fate.

For, silent lie all dusty graves, and mute,
As does the ash of a funeral pyre—
If was peeled off a prince in regal suit,
Or off a pauper that died a death dire;
For death when comes, comes equal— in all faith,
Levelling all— if not in life, in death!

- Sonnets | 01.11.11 |

$E=mc^2$

The egg ne'er dies; lives on in worm's new spell,
Nor does voracious worm when shedding skin—
O to make hardy hospitable shell,
To grow wings butterfly to be within;
And soon the wings as well wither away—
Manure to be for plants that pollens bloom,
That, new wings may feed on nectar one day,
And lay eggs new cycles of life to groom;
Or take a frozen snowflake, icy chunk,
A dank droplet of water or hot steam,
They transform keeping cool face of a monk,
Naught e'er dies a vain death, so to me seem!
>   *What's death save an eternal, endless cycle*
>   *Of change; a lazy thought ever so idle!*

Is not death of life like a quantum change— say, from energy to matter? It is an eternal, ever-changing cycle. When the contents of an egg become a worm, say caterpillar, it is only transformation, no death. It's again the same when the worm transforms into butterfly. Only, some changes are not so visible.

- Sonnets | 04.11.11 |

Fair or unfair, life's there

I might ill fate it call, lame luck or chance,
Others the law of seeds and whimsy sprouts,
And yet others, destiny's dappled dance,
Sitting on fence, ruminating old doubts;
Yet, karma clings to catch up with the life,
Dishing out platefuls of choicest fortune,
Or a life of frustration, sour fruits rife,
Darkling rainy clouds or sunshine of June;
Existence lives along with providence,
Life like a river flows as is meant to,
And little cares to leave behind some sense,
Nor master print leaves— blueprint, nor a clue;
    Life scarce moves straight, but traces curves in space,
    And not e'en an atom seems out of place[1].

---

1. The last line paraphrases what Swami Vivekananda said: 'Not even an atom in this universe can be different than how it is, for that would destroy the balance of the universe and the entire system would collapse.' Indeed, the so-called destiny's whims and frustrations caused by fate seem to be part of the universal creed; it is due to this observed unfairness that we see the much-needed continuity. Imagine if things changed as per every individual's desire, wishes and wants, and as per every caprice and fancy; the chaos and the confusion would have long consumed all the cosmos. Remember, even chaos has at its core some method in madness.

- Sonnets | 09.11.11 |

The race is still to the swift

Sad, happy, but long being life's journey
And heavy the burden men should carry,
O slow down that steps you take be steady,
That, you may stumble not in a hurry;
An old Buddhist wisdom sensing this said;
Be steady and firm like a mountain wall,
And deep like ocean, mild like moon to stead,
Echoed Jain thought; it matters none at all
How slow ye walk long as ye walk the way,
Confucius creed thence came to mankind's aid,
In much hurry man may well go astray,
So, slow down to a stone, and reach un-sped,
    Beware; Christ's race was never to the swift,
    And yet, the world still races to the lift!

The world seems to be in frantic hurry despite all spiritual wisdom. There's rat race in every field. See, how while driving a car we push ahead of others; how we rush breaking the queue the moment the lift arrives; how we rush to alight the train that may have been delayed for hours.

- Sonnets | 02.12.11 |

Spirituality

Contents

Dharma is one quart

Ancient shritis[1] and smriris[2] rage,
There's no one thinker sage
Whose words weigh, be a standard gauge;
If truth of dharma, its reality
Dwells deep, in my heart's cavity,
What the path-finders showed,
Let that path be followed.

There is one truth buried within,
There's one religion, one belief
That renders feeling hearts relief,
Varied be the ways they are seen;
Dharma makes but one quart,
The rest if is no heart,
It's all art of the mart.

---

1. Shritis: In Indic philosophy the divine scriptures like Vedas, considered as given. They are heard or read by the learned.

2. Smritis: Following from the foregoing, what remains in memories and **saṁskāras** (subtle, sublime impressions that survive from birth to birth).

The first stanza highlights the underlying theme of a verse in Mahabharata— **shṛtir vibhinnā** . . .

-Musings | 07.12.14 |

The kernel of truth

What suffers the body be and mind,
Reach the roots, everything left behind,
If Father and I be only one,
Everything is— under high heaven,
Fruit's not far should we rid all the rind.

When asked what the cause and cure of all sufferings in world could be, a sage responded: Find out 'who' is suffering. This limerick, which unlike their genre is thought-provoking, does throw some light.

-Reflections | 06.12.14 |

Search is all, path the end

You are an undying distant promise,
A slow traveller I'm on foot,
Suffering separation for long,
Dissipating, to die on the way,
Seeing no end of the endless path;
In getting I lose thee,
In losing I deem my gain;
An endless quench and death of death,
Let this long discontent be life.
In darkling clouds His radiant outline
Comes to be and goes off the sight,
Which, I can't in my eyes capture;
And that faint Him oft shows and goes off,
Which, in the illusion of moon's magic beam
I search in every grain of creation,
And scarce can recognise still.

From **mahāgītā** by Osho, in Hindi

- Translations | 20.08.14 |

Not death, it's faith in life

Ask him who has died still alive,
How often Death must strive,
Looking nigh somewhat naïve,
How long He should try to arrive.
Ask those for long alive,
Eternal as lives Death
Betwixt the birth and death,
Life living breath to breath,
Ask how oft he should strive.

My task it is spring-like to renew,
Recharge tired batteries anew,
Goes on while journey—searching, seeking rife.
Though there's no end past every life,
I do when come to call,
Life gets the same prison, same strife,
I change no more than wall;
O cross river of no return,
Let all walls fall, freedom to earn.

And while I try, life goes on as aught,
Triumphing o'er me to shine,
Not Death, the winner's Faith!
So, while rocks turn to sands, and sands to naught,
The wheel of Time[1] as turns, things wrought,
Man tries— as I with pen of mine,
Nary a care of next breath,

Nor of liberating death,
O thinking just of next line!

---

1. In Sanskrit the word **kāla** denotes both time and death. Here,
    Time and Death both mean the same.

Not death, nor breath (life), what triumphs is faith: a serious thought,
but the piece has a tongue-in-cheek end.

- Musings | 01.08.14 |

Religions

Cadavers of forgotten truth
Captured long ere in ancient age,
Kept imprisoned in golden cage,
And e'er since dead—dead in their youth,
Truth, few tried to digest, work with,
Much less realised or relished,
Now to the masses as is dished
Out as assorted myth;
Truth in its metered, footed beauty,
Every word captured as was heard,
Each singing like rarest of bird,
Looking winsome in captivity;
Its truth remaining still much blurred,
Behind bars, imprisoned, unheard!

And men not quite in search of knowledge,
Forget can scarce the golden cage,
Nor can transcend its beauty's rage,
Prisoner of every word bare,
From age to age eager to share,
The same long-rotting cadaver
That he fondly calls religion.
Bequeathed to each generation,
Promising for hereafter, heaven,
Each losing an essence from core,
Each getting rotten a tad more,
Ever the worse than was before,
Perhaps why religions so much smell,

Few knowing this still, such is their spell
For followers— frogs in a well
That reason with their heart, not head,
Having tonnes of hate and hatred
In green or white, or shades of red!

No, religion has ever opened doors,
Nor has it led believers safe to shores.
If religion born is from fears that grow,
As God invented was from loose ends,
How can pure nectar from it flow?
How'd oil drip from desert's dry sands?

But where, where's the escape?
There seems no deliverance from this rape
Of faith, as truth first enters head,
Appreciated, enjoyed, though dead,
Ere can reach a long waiting heart,
And stay there for many a birth
Before proving its worth;
Is there a way apart?

- Satire | 05.07.14 |

The journey is the joy

Thou art an undying distant promise,
Me a slow traveller on foot
Suffering separation for long,
Dissipating to die on the way,
I see when no end of the endless path.
In getting I lose thee,
In losing I seem to gain,
Let this long discontent be life—
Endless quench, death of death.
In darkling clouds thine lightning outline
Comes to be and soon goes off the sight,
That I can't in eyes capture,
The faint thee oft showing, as oft lost,
Which in the illusion of the moonbeam,
I search in every grain of creation,
And scarce can still recognise.
I travel, discontent my life,
Yet, journey is my joy.

From **mahāgitā** in Hindi by Osho

- Translation | 12.07.14 |

Karmic Tax

On filing up tax returns one late night,
Preparing I was to sleep sound in peace,
And heard a strange voice hailing me,
Prying op my eye-lids heavy with sleep,
Introducing him as Chitragupta,
Whom I knew as a Book-keeper in Chief
At the highest no-appeal court of Death.
Demanded he: Have ye paid up all tax?
Well in advance—and tax paid off at source,
Duly deducted from my salary,
I answered feeling proud, self-satisfied.
Not quite, my friend, my books show a loose ending,
How can my tax ever outstanding be?
A tad hesitated, irritated,
I asked rubbing my tired sleep-deprived eyes.

O for a night-long daily peaceful sleep,
Pay back ye must by helping someone sleep;
For golden sun rays, dew drops every dawn,
You pay by spreading light in someone's darkling life;
Providence has fragrance of flowers spread
In your life breath that haply you may live.
Is not it debt 'pon your oblivious head?
Should not ye soften someone's strife?
A learned man you are and ye should know,
Think of all debts outstanding, unpaid still,
Think of obligations staring at you,
And they would keep staring till you pay.

Taken have you things given and granted,
That in my books tagged I've in bold and red,
Remember, there's naught whatso owned by thee—
Rain is not, nor is sun—coming for free,
Pay up in time penalty to avoid,
And we charge a surcharge and a cess too,
Long have ye free supply of fruits enjoyed
Sans sowing seeds, doing labour as due,
Sow best of seeds, better still sacrifice,
Or else loaded shall be your Karmic dice,
A sacrifice is self-paid advance tax,
Pay up ere deadlines go past max.

So saying he bang-closed his book,
While I woke up rubbing my eyes,
And wearing a tax-dodger's look,
Felt somewhat penitent and wise.

- Reflections | 02.01.13 |

The now is all I have

I saw a yellowing brown leaf
That filled me with moments of grief,
And mind went to spring that had been,
To riots of shades tender green.

And when I saw an old leaf fall,
One, two, and then a virtual rain,
I felt: while autumn's here again,
Vain is to think far be the fall.

And what Kalidasa[1] once said
Came to my memory still red:
Yesterday is but a spent dream,
Morrow a vision— gay or grim,

Today if lived to fullest brim,
Makes yesterday a happy dream;
Now is the moment to cherish,
And thing to relish as sole wish!

The past has spent up all its now,
The morrow too shall come and how,
I may live to rue my lost now,
Passing moment's all I've to love.

Let me live for no other scene,
Morrows have vague vision unseen,
Autumns or falls, have varied charms,
Nature hugs them all, open arms.

---

1.   Kalidasa: A celebrated poet of sixth century AD, who wrote **abhijñāna shākuntal**, **raghuvaṁsha**, **kumāra saṁbhava**, **meghadūta**, **ṛtu saṁhāra**, and many other works.

- Musings | 08. 03.13 |

We like what's not

If seasons tell me in one voice,
Rejoice in Nature's every mood,
There's no choice— life's lent to rejoice—
Failing to see truth I still brood.
Spring comes on wings of scented breeze
To gladden every living heart,
Straighten forehead's long frozen crease,
Give my life push for a new start;
Summer fetches boons dresst as banes,
Nature packs gains disguised as pains;
Marveling earth, spreading splendour,
Monsoon comes with mystic grandeur;
Autumn schools: all things one day fall,
Fall, to get up, gather, grow tall,
Call it taxing time, boon or balm,
Winter comes, spreads peculiar charm.

And still a fool of faulty school,
I always want whatso be naught,
Wanting it warm when weather's cool,
Greed neighbour's greener-looking plot—
Gardens giving green proof with grin
That envy is dyed tempting green!

The first stanza is inspired by a few verses from ***Sāma Veda***. Man is more often than not unhappy with the passing season, and finds faults with it rather than seeing the fair side. He seems more comfortable with yesterday, even the morrow, than with the fleeting, melting present moment.

- Musings | 05.04.13 |

How squirrels earned their stripes

No man's too small to hail a helping hand,
Nor is there a deed too small if well meant,
No task howso tough is too hard to fend,
Mind if not flesh can make a goodly dent.

And a journey of thousand miles and more
Begins with but a single step forward,
Drop by drop fills up lake is no lore,
An ounce of action . . . yea, we all have heard.

Many a learned man know this truth well,
Who'd quote than contribute, ho hum and hypes,
Intent's what matters in life; a squirrel
It was that strived and earned her distinct stripes.

So goes a tiny squirrel's tallest lore,
Who, silent did work building up a ledge—
An episode from an epic of yore,
So sang sage Valmiki1 of ancient age.

A folktale aside from Ramayana:
Rama's innocent spouse whilst in exile,
In lonely woods and lone, whom Ravana,
Kidnapped, disguised as was in a monk's guile.

Ah, chasing the lure of a golden deer,
Which, too was a demon's bewitching guile,
Who, in stealth cried out, 'Lakshman, O my dear',
And destiny unfolded in a while.

Harvest of the Late Season

In Rama's voice the wily demon cried,
Sita beseeching Lakshman, forcing him
To render help, what followed far too grim,
For, restive Ravan waited in monk's hide.

The quest begins thence in woods and deep vales,
Hilly terrains, meadows and leas and dales,
And they come searching to where ends the land,
An ocean spread forth looking like no friend.

Hanuman, Rama's key aid, an ape hand,
To whom no task too big was, yon of him,
Then volunteers to leap across the land,
Alluring Lanka, land of golden dream!

And he returns with a goodly sad tale:
Sita's safe but captive, Ravan's red hand,
In no mood fair peace parleys to avail,
Demons aught be defeated in their land.

Rama pleads with the Lord of Sea to give way,
Adamant yet, when he was hard to melt,
Made he was wise reason failing to pay,
Ere long when a challenging threat was dealt.

Rama begins then building a bridge 'pon sea,
To deal with demons impervious to plea,
Apes lumber rocks, coughs a tiny squirrel
Keen to contribute if but a trickle,

Bestirred, she gets busy, boastful the least,
Running errands; look at this tiny beast!
Struggling hard to figure what to do,
A noble task it was Ma Sita to rescue.

Wet, she wallowed in the coastal dry sand,
To sea again, leaping from stone to stone,
Unloading tiny grains ere returning to land,
The monkeys and bears tickled to their bone.

Far too busy was she way above all,
What with fun, funny bone, work worship was,
Sacred comes every task, naught is too small,
It's value, not volume, to noble cause.

And Rama watchful of it all amidst,
Said, wiping tears of joy welling in eyes,
'Ah, my tiny soldier, ne'er yet the least',
Happy he sure was this to realize:

'There's not a doubt I'd meet my beloved spouse,
'Defeat demons all, mighty be or mouse',
So saying he lifted the smallest wonder,
The monkey brigade as raised a loud thunder.

And placed this spirit-lifter in his palm,
Soldiers as sang paeans of praise, sweet psalm,
Soothing with fingers her ruffled wet furs,
Ere what was grey turned fairy stripes of hers.

Squirrels come with stripes since that olden day,
A tale of fair intent, no tithe in tray!

---

1. Valmiki: Ramayana was written by him, a sage who was a fierce bandit in his early age.

- Drama | 06.04.13 |

Musings of a masked man

'He that sees all beings in self his own,
'And sees his self reflecting in all still',
That, empathy and brotherhood to all
As Krishna taught, I may here feel.

But let me give a boon of doubt—
Good start to journey ahead lined,
If I can't all on my way love,
Let me learn to be tad more kind.

As Gandhi deemed it too distant
A goal to get, fit for a saint,
I watered down goals to bare skin:
O least to be nigh tolerant.

Yet, being in competing world,
Where, kind might be too weak a word,
Hands held high, white flag a fluttered,
Conceded I, ere case was heard.

There's no Eros[1] without Agape[2,]
Nor is Agape if no Eros,
He's love, nor kindness who's no strong,
One more problem popped up to pose.

Being strong too is no mean task,
I find it hard to mask my mask.

---

1. Earthly or sensual love, god of love, Cupid.
2. Used here in the sense of brotherly love, charity.

- Tongue-in-cheek | 10.04.13 |

This too shall sooner pass

As one old brownish yellow leaf
Fell, another followed and more.
The tree shed still no tears of grief,
Even as autumn came ashore,
It held her faith firm from heart's core,
So firm in spring was her belief;
In every green sprout, every leaf,
In every tender blade of grass,
A throbbing life did silent roar,
Telling, this too shall sooner pass!

- Musings | 13.04.13 |

I thought of asking God

I once thought of asking God,
Why He's the world made so odd—
A goodly Him and kind Lord;
Why He lets poverty be,
Injustice all 'round we see,
Men in mires of misery,
More yet still that need not be;
And why He takes none to task;
But scarce could bring it on board,
Afraid, he'd in return ask:

To thine cavils— isn't the cob thee?
To thine queries the cause is thee.
Think, why plain things profound be,
No straight answers come in cask,
What use is it— me to ask?
Thou maketh thy world, thine task.

- Musings | 01.08.13 |

You God and me

At times I see thee as guru thou art,
And me as thine minuscule part,
See thee as great master, a vehicle,
And me a fumbling disciple;
In company of precious diamond,
I thought me a carbon— not but coal;
Oft I see thee as ocean, pole-to-pole,
And me but a land-locked stagnant pond;
Lost amid an infinite whole,
And find me struggling, puny soul.

But when I know the truth well and how,
I find that thou art I, and me thou,
Thou art a complete whole,
And me too a complete whole,
One whole born from another whole,
Should one, one from the 'ther remove,
One whole would still remain— and all of love.
Unable my potential still to see,
Here am I, a struggling me,
Stranded, feeling helpless, mid-sea!

- Musings | 05.08.13 |

Bliss is in being

Hi, how are you?
I'm fine is his view.
But is he?
None can 'become' happy,
Who, happy simply 'is',
For, being is bliss,
Just to be,
And be so as seasons come,
As it rains, the winds as blow,
The buds as blossom,
The greens and grass as grow,
And under the sunny heaven,
All things as ordained happen.

Yet, in this 'becoming' world,
Where are you O happy bird?

- Reflections | 01.09.13 |

Lost in search

Easy to know nor spell nor yet sound,
Nor far still and if lost seldom found,
Pen fancied promises no good hand,
With fancied epithets still off bound,
No use long search, nor go round and round,
When so close you seem, ever around,
No wonder scriptures[1] were on weak ground,
Tired sniffing you out when like a hound,
So when journey ends of a thousand
Tries too far, begins search inward-bound.

---

1. Indic scriptures try to define atman by the allusion: *neti, neti,*
    for it is hard to pin point what it is, and easier what it is not.

- Musings | 07.09.13 |

And life has never been the same

A thorn as thorn to flower once said:
Anyone can crush you, no care,
And wordless as if mute you bear,
Far too timid hast God you made;
Look, none would mess with me, nor dare.
Sure, none can be more right, my friend,
Said flower, but you won't understand,
Look, my life for others is meant,
For others hast dear God me sent,
Seeing me dance, dance they with joy,
Pluck and pick me, even destroy,
And yet, that is my life's sole joy;
But, seeing you they turn away,
The reason your colour is grey,
Short, but life should make someone's day.

And e'er since thorns have changed their game,
Protecting buds and shoots as came,
What ere was shame now gives good name,
And their life has ne'er been the same!

- Musings | 01.12.13 |

To my mind

A rudder-less ship on high seas,
Ye ride on wings of wish horses;
Stay tuned to heart,
To get good start,
Stay still and soon the storm shall cease.

- In Prayer | 01.02.11 |

Stirrings of soul

Searching, seeking I took to sail
And spent my life's prime to its trail,
In circles moved on un-mapped sea,
Looking afar unknown to see,
But returned in vain a tired bone,
And found as teacher house my own,
When I hugged him, he said:
'What lies far is faded,
'O Seek not and search not,
'There lies o'er-flowing inner pot.'

***

I saw a sage starving, in death, disease,
I saw a fool felling the tree that sheltered him,

A brown leaf afloat in a rainy breeze,
A wise man chasing his weird dream,
I saw men of power pinned by puny thoughts,
Saw, learned men slavish to lucky slots;
I want now to go with that winging bird—
But something keeps me tied to this vain world.

***

I tried whatso books that me teach,
Searched and sought to self preach,
Lived fighting inner fiends as aught,
It taught me well, taught me a lot,
For I preached one thing not
O doing another uncaught.

***

I wandered far to seek Nature's soul—
Climbed many a weary mountain peak,
Tried, break from many a mundane goal,
And so hoped my soul one day to seek,
In fond hope that uncalled it may call.

***

I rushed and rushed against the time,
And spent my youth, all my life's prime;
Old age came, slowed me down,
Things I sought came to town;
Patience friend till prime ripens the time.

- Stirrings | 01.07.11 |

In addition, there are poems elsewhere in this book that are on spirituality. For instance there are many sonnets on this theme. Here is a list.

1. No use in shallows to swim   Sonnets | 03.12.14 |
2. Rejoice, the soul is alive   Sonnets | 15.12.14 |
3. Be thy own light   Sonnets | 22.08.14 |
4. Disillusion is when bliss   Sonnets | 07.06.14 |
5. Keep no monkey at bay   Sonnets | 05.02.14 |
6. To learn from every turn   Sonnets | 05.01.14 |
7. The four that think of me   Sonnets | 12.04.13 |
8. Sonnets | 12.04.13 | Sonnets | 06.06.13 |
9. Mind be when no good maid   Sonnets | 08.06.13 |
10. O to know me   Sonnets | 09.06.13 |
11. Man cannot the big picture see   Sonnets | 07.07.13 |
12. The world unwilling to wake   Sonnets | 08.08.13 |
13. When God created man   Sonnets | 12.08.13 |
14. Life is a waiting room   Sonnets | 08.09.13 |
15. Faith   Sonnets | 01.10.13 |
16. Who are you?   Sonnets | 07.11.13 |
17. To see mother masking as Maya   Sonnets | 10.01.12 |
18. Death, tail-wind of change   Sonnets | 01.09.12 |
19. Whatso might happen happens . . .   Sonnets | 08.04.11 |
20. All nature seems to while time.   Sonnets | 14.07.11 |
21. Joy is the way   Sonnets | 05.08.11 |
22. O to live and let go   Sonnets | 02.09.11 |
23. Twain of paths trodden by men   Sonnets | 08.10.11 |
24. Fair or unfair, life's there   Sonnets | 09.11.11 |

Happenings, Humour

Contents

Pen, book, woman if lost

No one quite the moods of his pen knows,
Nor of book if read well or not shows,
Nor of wife weathered for lifetime close—
With thorns comes the fragrance of a rose.
    Be it pen, book or wife, moody goes,
    Pen pretends poetic oft to pose,
    Book dog-eared and much-nosed, few still knows,
    Nuances new show up in slow dose.
A common trait that everyone owes:
If ever in alien hand one goes,
Rare if it returns with a good nose,
    And if so, pen's dead if not diseased,
    The book used, misused, yet comes back missed,
    And woman if ravished not, much kissed!

This piece uses a nine syllabic anapaestic metre.

-Tongue-in-cheek | 02.12.14 |

No council without double-speak

There's no court with wise old not well lined,
Nor yet old to dharma that be blind,
None of whom would vouch truth
Not hidden hind a booth,
There's no truth not with tricks un-entwined.

Elephants we know have teeth to chew and those to show and combat with. But this is the fact of life. The path of dharma is not easy to define. Sage Vyasa wrote a biggest ever epic of Mahabharata on this theme. Bheeshma, Drona, Vidura, and other old guards fumbled facing the truth posed by Draupadi, and admitted they were slaves to their self interests— **arthasya dāsaḥ ahaṁ**. Today's assemblies are housed by Dhritarashtras more than the truly wise. So we know what to expect.

-Happenings | 04.12.14 |

Travel costs and four-play

Two is twain and more no crowd today,
Nor be four a crazy lot all gay,
But a good company,
'Tis honeymoon, Honey;
My hope— this four-play mars no fore-play!

A travel survey recently found a staggering 70% of couples preferring to be accompanied by another couple. Now, don't giggle, nor snigger. This is only aimed at bringing down travel costs. But my hope is: see the piece.

-Happenings | 09.12.14 |

Poor Jack, down the hill

One must bend knees climbing up a hill,
So is approaching one's wedded Jill;
Jacks do jog from times old,
Yet, says she shoulder cold,
'No, I'm not placated enough still!'

Many a much harassed husband might have climbed this conjugal hill trying to please, especially after a tiff with his spouse, and yet cold-shouldered like this Jack.

-Humour | 10.12.14 |

Flies and mouths unbuttoned

Mice, nor microbes of a million grade,
Nor sundry parasites we so dread,
But fools harm that much strut,
And scarce can keep mouths shut,
We know flies, mouths unzipped do filth spread!

Union minister Sadhvi Niranjan Jyoti, by her controversial remarks, a tongue let loose, created uproar in the House disrupting proceedings. (using words Ramzade and Haramzade). The words do not befit a *sadhvi* (that's what she calls herself). Besides she is a minister and elected member of the House. But fools venture where the wise shudder to go. This limerick talks of those that can't keep traps shut.

-Happenings | 16.12.14 |

My bad, too bad

Move over 'I am fine', here's 'I'm good',
'Sorry seems prude; 'my bad' time's new mood,
Semantic upheaval,
Spirit of time and will,
But old fashioned can't eat this junk food.

The internet has gunned down many a kosher phrase and flagged-in those that academic camps would have frowned at. But youth has invaded every field and the world seems to have stood up-side down. 'I'm fine' in response to 'how are you' is too old. It's now 'I'm good'. Similarly, 'I'm sorry' also is too old, and 'my bad' has replaced it. 'Like' has become a sort of verbal comma. What else? But wait, who are we to judge? It is the prevailing Zeitgeist, bow to it.

- Happenings/The ways of words | 01.10.14 |

Night of nude knives

Gracefulness goes under, greed arrives,
And queen bees get driven out of hives,
Basal, oft one rung-adder
Be young ambition's ladder,
In what Saffron night was of nude knives!

Packed off to pastures green

The party might well show goodly gesture,
Everyone had his oft-crushed conjecture:
Speaker-ship, mentorship,
Viral went the guess ship,
Lost was he— from green lea to dry pasture.

What happened in many a political party has now happened to the new ruling party, with old stalwarts eased out of the Parliamentary Board. Old age has for long been respected in Indian culture. The reign of old age prevailed in this party as elsewhere. But times it seems are a changing. Perhaps, age should know when her time is up. The two limericks above highlight the underlying mood.

- Happenings | 02.09.14 |

Sitar suppressed

What the world guessed for long got the voice:
A gifted wife had had no fair choice;
And what the affront was?
Louder she drew applause!
Sad, ego played spoil-sport to world joys.

There were inklings, and hushed up tunes in musical circles, and the world for decades had wondered. What was guessed has now got the voice. The sitar maestro, Ravi Shankar's first wife Annapurna Devi, his guru's daughter, has now admitted that she retired from public life because her husband didn't like that she drew forth more applause than him. How sad! A gifted sitar has gone muted, silent but singing still.

- Happenings | 05.09.14 |

Captain crazy

He knows how biting bouncers to bowl,
To cool rivals who in pressure crawl,
There's pace, guile, seam and swing,
And Yorkers toe-crushing,
Generals thence too keen, called foul, foul!

Let democracy be damned. Pakistan's Tehreek-i-Insaf (PTI) chief, Imran Khan, former cricket captain, has always relished tormenting his rivals with pace bowling. He still continues in similar vein, now joined by a cleric, Qadri. Connived at by the army, he has pushed back Prime Minister Nawaz Sherif.

The captain was instrumental in winning the 1992 ODI World Cup, and thinks 'Naya (new) Pakistan' can be built without concrete plans. What so be, who so wins, the people of Pakistan might lose the match in the end.

- Happenings | 06.09.14 |

Security in cloud

Hackers see thru an unguarded cloud,
And guarded shrouds dance singing aloud;
Smart frontiers face hazards
Undreamt by the web guards,
Clouds are clouds capricious— quite like crowd.

Hackers ferret out private photos, nude and all, of some glitterati's in show business, kept in cloud computing sites, a routine practice now. But crooks seem to be smarter than smart phones, their users, and service providers, all put together.

- Happenings | 07.09.14 |

I've no promises to keep

Son shows ere arriving at the shore,
And daughter-in-law right at the door,
Politicians aver,
But never deliver
Promises promised, packed well before!

The first by-election was indicative enough. Poor voting of less than 50 per cent for the second, and the result that followed showed that people's enthusiasm had waned. The hundred days in office have hardly helped people keep their hopes alive. They now wonder if a barrage of verbose promises during electioneering would be fulfilled. Yet, the promised good days are nowhere here nor are in horizon.

-Happenings | 11.09.14 |

Poll, a punishing pole

And after the landslide, there's a slide,
A bride won, but honeymoon denied,
Much wonted charm on wane,
Patience as ends in pain,
Promises made, performance belied.

This is what the third consecutive by-election seems to say on the ruling party's performance. A lot of promises were made during parliamentary elections. People tired of erstwhile regime's pathetic performance gave the alternative a landslide victory. But after more than 100 days the regime has little to show on the promises made, people's patience wearing thin. No wonder, the poll has turned a punishing pole.

-Happenings | 12.09.14 |

If only one learns

History oft has lessons to teach,
If one's keen to learn, life to enrich,
No lasting live winners,
Nor losers nor sinners,
But bridges aught be built ere we reach.

Victory wears hard on men, and the party in power is no exception. Forming the government is not too hard. It is the performance, stupid, good governance, and delivery on promises made.

- Happenings | 13.09.14 |

He came when

The city is decked up like a bride,
Riverfront roars, squalor on the hide,
For, mega billions lure,
Safe borders to endure,
When we hide I wonder where's the pride?

I was there the day Chinese dignitaries came. The city was virtually under siege. Traffic was blocked and people were barred on many roads, even peeping from balconies as alleged. There were huge screens blocking the view of squalor— of poor people in huts. The riverfront was vacated save VIPs. And Gujarati papers talked of **asmitā**, meaning fond pride!

- Happenings | 14.09.14 |

When he left

Left, leaving dollar dreams still unsigned,
Inscrutable a smile well behind,
His soldiers staying put,
With arms and army boot,
Borders still disputed, ill defined.

And yet, the expected hundred billion dollars were nowhere. The pressure on the borders was especially mounted, and no talks on settlement. What earlier was 100 billion dollars has now shrunk to twenty over five years, all pledged and loosely promised and subject to conditions galore. He left, leaving us guessing and on tenterhooks, gulf at the borders staring still as before.

- Happenings | 15.09.14 |

Loo before you leap

So, let me look before I should leap.
'Loo before' ah seems a good belief,
Closer is cleanliness
To godliness I guess,
And bottoms up as well as a brief!

The new PM's Independence Day speech was marked by two block-buster announcements: Kicking out the Planning Commission, kicking in the toilets-first policy— loo before leaping to new frontiers.

- Happenings | 07.08.14 |

Words spoken and not

Inner voice, sacrifice, you may quote,
Quote too I care no chair, let them note,
(Sotto voce):
Let someone warm the chair,
Let him throne of thorns bear,
And haply dance still to my remote!

The veil is lifting at last. First it was Sanjay Baru, who exposed truth in his book, 'The Accidental Prime Minister'; and now it is Natvar Singh shedding light on the remote control that was. Forget the halo carefully created; forget 'inner voice', and the air of renunciation and sacrifice— a case of power without accountability, to be a king-maker than king.

This limerick imagines what the lady at the helm might have thought through in her mind—sotto voce and aloud.

- Happenings | 18.08.14 |

Gym, a new route to divorce

Fighting flab, nor keeping on health tabs,
Nor yoga to tone up sagging abs,
Gym for aside affair
With fitness trainer there,
A new route to divorce, lab of labs!

Husband busy with business of money: away, uninterested, or incapable; and wife, 'for fitness, honey'! Gymnasiums and yoga training centres come to help neglected wives. The fitness trainer is young, fit, suave, and receptive. The forcing flab also needs urgent attention. All make up for a good fuel for an impending fire. Yes, gyms are new labs and a short route to divorce.

- Happenings | 24.08.14 |

Rip Van Winkle

Caught was he dosing off in the House,
Laymen kept while vigil with grey grouse,
Yet, is not there a plan
Ever since it began?
Sleepy all day night-hectic goes mouse.

It's not Rahul alone. We have had a dosing PM, and snoring ministers, MPs browsing on blue sites, even absent, late-coming, sleepy public servants in most government offices. Have not they all been dosing for the last six and half decades? If not, how can we be in such a mess? How can our problems go out of control? How can our work ethics be so awful?

One can't help feel there has been a plan to keep the public asleep so that leaders can keep their eyes closed. May be, there have been calculated moves to keep the masses uneducated as well so that votes can be had from drowsy sheep; plan to keep them poor and in need so that votes can be bought. A ruling party has been punished in recent elections, and a new one is in power. Though it is too early to judge good days are unlikely.

- Happenings | 02.07.14 |

A school for the fools

Ah, what a varsity down the town!
Fools where frolic flaunting folksy crown,
Where bright and nerdy wise,
May seldom get a prize,
Domes that keep you grounded if not down.

Daddarpada Vishva Vidyalaya, Chitradurga, in Karnataka, India. Leading the team and the idea is a man who calls himself 'dumbest of them all', yet a pillar of folk music. He never got past class one in school. A school dropout, he wandered around the State exploring abundant folk practices and travelled as many as 29, 343 villages, and given 12,508 stage shows, sharing the rich traditions of folklore. The five year course at the university will have less theory and more practical lessons covering some 64 disciplines.

Why such a university? The present system of education, he feels, is aimed at filling the stomach, and not the soul. The course content centres on these five tenets:

- **shrama**, i.e., labour, efforts
- **krama**, order, sequence, priority
- **pari-shrama**, perseverance
- **parākrama**, valour, and
- **vikrama**, victory.

I can't but agree more, and suggest reading another poem 'Go add to the beauty of life', | 08.07.14 |.

- Happenings | 09.07.14 |

Greed is good

If well off we're than were,
Why's jolly Joe still a broody Bill?
Why's a smiling face rare?
The more one has the more he wants still,
O thankless puffing up a steep hill!

Matt Ridley in his book, The Rational Optimist, sounds temptingly good and valid too. He seems to say: Greed is good. I hope it follows an inverted U curve. If so, how much of greed is greed; and how much is need? Humanity at a future point will have to decide this. Yet, Destiny alone has the big picture; and knows what is good for us. So, let us be optimists, rational or not.

-Happenings | 10.07.14 |

Poems: a bit like baking cakes

Call it Muse or mood or attitude—
Search of good ending in fodder food,
I wonder when I wake
If it's like baking cake:
No matter what some cakes turn no good!

Even proven among poets at times turn out pieces that are forgettable at best. I often wonder if penning poems is like baking cakes. No matter what you do some will turn out no good, call it muse, mood, or attitude.

- Tongue-in-cheek | 03.06.14 |

Poetry and politics

Something sets me this ponder hard—
Poetry if pumps up politics,
Or politics trumps poetics—
I've seen many that see them as bard,
And some rhymesters and no more
That manoeuvre with just an oar.

Take this now out-of-job minister[1],
Another, if I may, rhymester,
Palming out puerile rhymes,
Who thought poet he was ahead of times,
And claimed that he meditated
Thru poems and earned his grade.

Here is one more known for some valour,
Reciting times in gilded glamour,
And captive audience claps his fame.
One more writes verses of some value,
Reflecting in his chair's borrowed hue,
Who, could have stood well on his name[2].

Technology now a pen-pusher aids,
It takes now pressing a few keys,
And lines come to life, so much ease,
A jacinth jostling with odd jades,
Juggling with gems of varied shades,
If pen-pusher a smart poet is.

165

I'm no Plato poets to hate,
Yet, politicians I do lowly rate.
So, I feel of this fairly sure:
Poetry often seem to lure
The 'ther, but seldom is richer made,
Nor can politics earn a better grade.

---

1.   One of his gems:
     30 days, 84 Tweets, /They say I've reached over 2 cr peeps, As I am
     on this medium sold, /I gather all that twitters isn't gold,/ Here I
     gather plenty insights, /From politics to basic rights.
2.   Both were once Prime Ministers in India.

- Satire | 04.06.14 |

Bananas to keep gold lure at bay

Bananas, traditional time-ticked way,
That came, Customs to bale,
Laxatives did when fail.
An apple if keeps doctors away,
The lay fruit, lo, keeps gold lure at bay.

Nine smugglers who flew in from Malaysia to India had earlier ingested 89 gold biscuits, and Customs forced them to give up their stash. The doctors when called in failed, failed when sundry laxatives, they tried plain old bananas. And lo and behold, the fruits of their labour were gleaming!

- Happenings | 06.06.14 |

Dictator is no dictater

What prevails be when custom, no rule,
The tail wags as a much tinkered tool,
Free for all reigns the rule,
And free-spell the sole school,
When spirit of time wills feel free, cool!

Suffixes (the tail) now matter no more. Noun formation from a verb with a suffix at the end (whether it should be an –er or –or) these days hardly matters, and either seems good enough. So, impostor becomes imposter; protester becomes protestor; most advisers are now advisors; supervisers, supervisors; yet sailors, sailers; and jailers, jailors. Even the difference between dictator and dictater has vanished. Little can be done if custom crashes and no rule reigns.

- Happenings (Ways of words) | 02.05.14 |

Fighting or feigning tears

Found was he fighting tears fizzing by,
It can't be too rehearsed a feigned try;
We shall soon have a clue,
That the tears teemed up true,
If he wipes tears from nation's sad eye!

The new PM entered Parliament House apparently overcome by emotions. Bowing on the steps he was found fighting moist eyes, a rare sight indeed. Let us take the gesture on the face value, although people we know do wear masks.

- Happenings | 04.05.14 |

Grand old party that was

Old for sure, no more good nor yet grand,
Flavour lost, now tasting a tad too bland,
King cobra has just passed,
Dead skin so dear un-cast,
Hood and hiss, hard put still to defend.

The so-called Grand Old Party is in dismal shape after poles. And yet the old stiffness is intact. Not in touch with realities, it is likened in this ditty to an old cobra: defanged and badly mauled.

- Happenings | 07.05.14 |

A prayer if prices rise

Nor hawkish nor yet downright dovish,
I'd call my policy nigh owlish—
Owl-like watchful and wise;
But why then prices rise?
Whilst hawks soar, vultures roam to relish!

The RBI Governor, Raghuram Rajan would like to call his policy at controlling inflation 'owlish', watchful and wise like an owl—neither hawkish, nor dovish. But with the government doing little to implement other measures, can inflation be fought solely on monetary policies? And what does the government do on hoarders and profiteers? This way we neither get growth nor curb greed.

- Happenings | 02.02.14 |

Global freeze

Polar winds showing strange, sudden quirk,
Northern world getting a frozen jerk,
Heavens, hell of this halt
Seems to say there's no alt
But to slow from too hectic a work!

A full circle from Global Warming to Global Freeze! For a world perennially on a rat-race mode, for rush-addicts that can't relax, there is a lesson to learn: Slow down and reflect. May be there still is time and a way to change. This is a Global Warning! Yet, this northern freeze seems to show, there always is a meeting ground. Even for two different thermal scales, Celsius and Fahrenheit, there is a meeting point, at minus forty degrees that some places have recorded.

- Happenings | 01.01.14 |

Good earth

God's the good earth made so fertile,
I wonder if need there's to toil,
Some ploughing here and probing there,
Watering, weeding nor yet care,
And lo, abundant crop should smile.

So, I tickled earth in some haste
To see, she laughs with rich harvest;
She did laugh but seemed not so pleased,
From a mild shock when I felt eased,
She said: you seem some sort of jest.

- Tongue-in-cheek | 07.01.14 |

In search of a cementing force

Ponderous pious words, way too meek,
But bulwarks of words are always weak,
Talks, talks, great goodly deal,
The words scarce walking still,
Barest bricks, cement too shy to stick!

BRICS: Brazil, Russia, India, China, and South Africa. With the other four members wary of the colossus China, her GDP of more than the combined sum of the remaining four, BRICS has not been able to make a marked progress ever since 2008, when the block came into being. The idea of BRICKS Bank, on the lines of IMF and World Bank, has also been a non-starter so far. The group perhaps is in search of a cementing force.

- Happenings | 07.04.13 |

On course to kiss disaster

A failed state, still no sense of remorse,
Nuke weapons far too-flogged, a tired horse,
Breathing by a live bomb
Ticking, trenched up in tomb,
Flaunting still a help-me-or-else force!

No riddle this nor a doubt, we are talking of Pakistan— no longer a cohesive State. They have for long arm-twisted USA, all the world, flaunting nuclear weapons: give us aid, free doles, us or else . . .

- Happenings | 08.04.13 |

To speak without a point

Forced to spell, compelled when to arrive,
Happy he's with honey from bee-hive,
Perhaps to prove, can speak,
Not yet what, when to pick,
But, 'arrived I've, am no more so naïve'!

Rahul Gandhi's speech at CII had most corporate chieftains chewing their pencils. He criticized the system of which his family has been at the helm. But if they were looking for solutions, they were naïve, not the speaker, who offered mere fables, homilies, parables, folk tales, and empty rhetoric. He likened India not with a ponderous elephant, but a beehive.

Shrewd metaphor to sidestep accountability! Beware, yet, if denied the honey, bees can turn on the queen bee. And too late it is for him to do a vision thing now at a fag end.

- Happenings | 09.04.13 |

Minister of unnatural gas

Ministers, well can talk royally,
Venting vainest rage not so coyly:
What they say oft is gas
Exposing verbal ass,
Should we boil over words so oily?

Some people just open their loud mouth and speak. So simple; they feel there's no need to think. The Union minister of Petroleum and Natural Gas seems to be one, who recently said: Petroleum ministers have been threatened by import lobbies. The country, he said, is floating in oil and gas, and still we have to import 80% of our requirement. Well, well, who is he complaining to? His ministry and the party in power should have done something about it. His predecessor Mr Ram Naik responded: 'A rider who complains about his horse is not a good rider.' One may be a minister of gas, but does he need to emit needless gas?

- Happenings | 07.06.13 |

Excuses

Planets on axes move to courses,
And life on cycles of birth and death,
Man alone can move on excuses,
Therein lies his fervent if false faith—
And hope he'd get away O with ease!

- Tongue-in-cheek | 01.07.13 |

Yes we can and also scan

If campaign one he said: yes we can,
In second seemed to say: we can scan,
Intelligence power is
Ignorance never bliss,
And spying was still there ere I ran.

US of A are trying to extradite Snowden, the contract agent of its intelligence agency, the man who had leaked a lot of secret documents to a whistle-blower site. Later he spilled further beans—America spying on EU and other friendly nations, apart from its own citizens. The US President said: Every intelligence service, not just ours, is trying to understand the world better. If not, it is of no use. This little ditty, a limerick, shows: in the game of politics, everyone gets coloured. Mark the degeneration from president's first campaign to the next.

- Happenings | 02.07.13 |

On discount

To dizzy heights green backs[1] ever mount,
And silver[2] scarce in count,
Rupee falls, showing tail,
Markets on the derail,
And country constant on cold discount!

---

1. Refers to US dollars
2. Refers to rupees,

From being at par and prime in 1947 (India's Independence), Rupee is today at 60 and more to the Dollar. Yet even now, if dollar dips RBI would rush to intervene in support. I'm no Economist, nor I know money matters much, but still feel, the country is being sold on discount.

- Happenings | 10.07.13 |

Bad-mean-ton

IPL wagging weight of a tonne,
Carnal kiss of commerce,
And money-minting curse,
Other sports on pointed-up a gun,
Where would be I wonder badminton?

Cricket started it all, thence followed boxing and hockey. The latest to join the band wagon is IBL, Indian Badminton League. Money has brought in ills as well as good things. Look at fixings and betting. Other sports' appetite is getting whetted and greed is considered good. Hope, badminton would remain good, if not turn one big bad-mean-ton.

- Happenings | 12.07.13 |

Green shoots

If they¹ that should talk of absolutes
Gamble for gossamer greener shoots,
If the road's wrought with roughs,
With no green but grey scruffs,
Pray, talk roots, or face people's poll boots.

---

1. They that should account for their acts of omission and commission, looking are for alibis and excuses!

'I am confident that the green shoots that are visible here and there will multiply and the economy will revive'.

> — FM, Chidambaram, Nov 15, 2013.

I am very encouraged by the indications of the green shoots in economy.

> — FM, Chidambaram, Dec 12, 2012.

'*Talk roots or face poll boots*', the limerick said. And with the hind sight, let me now say, they chose the later! - Aug 2014 ??

- Happenings | 06.11.13 |

Hearts, not parts

As many people as many arts,
Materials, merchandise, malls and marts,
And business this of love—
All equal, none above;
O make love; it's about hearts, not parts!

LGBTs[1] are in news; and anyone who is anybody is talking about the Supreme Court's verdict on the subject rejecting the earlier verdict of the Delhi High Court on article 377. I too and here am I with a limerick on the happenings.

1.   Lesbians, gay, bisexuals, and transsexuals.

- Happenings | 06.12.13 |

Backward boys but make noise

A softy banana has li'le voice,
The losers in this world have no choice
But to get felon's treat,
No use fuming with fit,
But backward boys no more than make noise.

India is no banana republic. Banish the thought, but it has hard lessons to learn from Devyani affair. The treatment meted out to her, an Indian consular official (whatso her fault), by the U.S. attorneys and police. The fact is: such a thing would not have happened to a Chinese or Russian civilian, forget one protected by Vienna convention for consular staff. We can take it as a wake-up call or go back to our forget-it ways as usual.

- Happenings | 07.12.13 |

And action born still

More coddled than paved, rusted than steel,
Caught in a frozen chill— peel o'er peel;
A Machiavellian maid
Moving no files till paid;
And action if born still is born still!

Indian bureaucracy gets a rating of 'worst in Asia' from a well-known consulting firm— a near-bottom rating, worse than for Vietnam, Indonesia, Philippines, and China. Not surprising since its inertia and red-tape can only be cured by goodly palm greasing. But why blame bureaucracy alone? What about our ministers, and elected representatives? Our polity in this land of Bhagavad-Gita and Krishna's teachings on karma, we are fond of talking more than acting. Note the pun on 'still' in the last line.

- Happenings | 01.01.12 |

The warp and weft of politics

A lady of letters of some heft,
Robbed of her wonted chill
Reacts with a question all so apt,
Lets out this bitter pill—
Why is she not in when Left has left?

"Media has been saying I was bundled out of West Bengal by the Left government. But (now that another government has taken over) they don't ask themselves: the Left is gone, then why can't I return."

— Taslima Nasreen, of Bangladesh, now in India, on politics of intolerance

---

- Happenings | 06.01.12 |

Serendipity of the century

'I tripped and fell into a life boat',
And for no reason made a scapegoat,
The ship captain cavilled
When on the mishap grilled;
Alibi of the year, what a quote!

"I tripped and ended up in one of the lifeboats'—Francesco, Costa Concordia captain, on why he abandoned his sinking cruise liner wherein many passengers died.

- Happenings | 07.01.12 |

Petticoat problems

Fair maidens; watch the stress on waistlines,
Pigments and scary scales, tell-tale signs;
Heed on how much to harden,
Tie and tighten, me pardon,
Which, not else but your own norm defines.

Tie your petticoat string loose; let it be a bit broader so that pressure on one spot is less; and Keep changing it. This is what doctors advise to avoid pigmentations and scaling leading to 'sari cancer'. But try advising anyone what and how to wear.

- Happenings | 11.01.12 |

Better lose hair than head

It's better to lose hair than my head,
Sacrifice butter than losing bread;
Yet, nothing in life's fair,
So thank my greying hair,
That head be, bare or bald, not yet dead!

-Tongue-in-cheek | 01.04.12 |

Her vegetable vendor

Her vegetable vendor's a nice man
Who she can spot from a long waiting mile,
Who welcomes as well with a weighty smile
That says, 'it's good to please and pamper my old fan'.
And then begin the bids, rounds of bargain
Designed all said and done to let her gain;
This done, returned are tomatoes too ripe,
Brinjals less brown and onions not her type,
And readily nigh well exchanges he,
Not once while his smile changes rehearsed glee.

But she likes him not for his mobile face,
Nor ever for his easy business grace,
Sweet chatter, soft words nor his ready smile,
Perhaps it is his cunning little guile
That seemingly— not in truth— lets her win
Without appearing to be so mean;
I suspect, he makes good the bargained price,
Weighing balance of his a loaded dice,
I too know his weights ne'er probity spell,
But such is his synthetic charming shell.

The deal's designed to make good her morning
That would all day long last, gaining a ring
Of a facile little win-win success,
Or so do I from goodly distance guess.

- Tongue-in-cheek | 02.05.12 |

Licence to bite

And he asked Shankar[1] ne'er him to spare,
Let cartoons of his as ever dare,
And blowers of power's blight
Cherished brush that did bite,
Cartoons should fumigate the false air.

---

1. A cartoonist among India's well-known trinity of greats:
    Shankar, R K Laxman, and Abu Abraham.

Time was when likes of Nehru encouraged cartoonists never to spare them with their critical brush. Today, politicians have moved a full circle, and cartoonists are dragged to courts for what they depict.

- Happenings | 04.05.12 |

Warmer still be my native womb

What a land, plateau, on lee side
Of world's tallest, coldest mountain,
Oldest, not uninhabited still, nor decried,
Facing the Central Asian plane,
Rain shadowed, scant south-west monsoon, most bare,
Dry, harsh desert, moisture nor rains,
Not but the sturdiest grass thriving there—
And tubers, carrots, radish, hardy grains.

Yet, like a colony of ants,
Does the land thrive on whatso the life grants,
Gathering victual the land makes,
Girls drying dung-made cakes,
Men folk chopping dry wood
To keep the winter warm and somewhat good,
Searching for an unknown faint reason
To live life in a twain of season—
Six months endeavouring to ensure,
That, the next six in struggle they endure.

September comes, crops are just right to greet,
And every house digs up a garden pit—
In time to bake it warm in summer heat,
O what with tubers, carrots, what be it,
Sealing it soon with straw,
Insulating with winter's snow—
An insurance against the frozen vows
Be these subterranean silos,

In snow the pass[1] gets frosty seal,
Hardest of Nature's harshest ill,
Power plants to pause when in unease,
And lively streams suffer when wintry freeze.

Life triumphs still and rises tall
Providence casts when an ugliest pall,
For, learnt have locals ingenious to be,
When water's frost, too stiff in pipes to flow,
They heat to keep them on and drippy—
All the water they need by melting snow;
They survive that know how to live,
When all birds beckon them to leave,
Migrating to warm, calibrated climes,
But alien lands awaiting better times.

People subsist still on meagre ration—
But not in hellish human hibernation—
For there is work to do,
Unpaid though, for incomes get frozen too:
'We must keep the stored water warm,
'And shovel snow from frozen roof,
'Cooking, cleaning, washing beside,
'And study when there's time aside',
Life does demand perennial proof,
They scarce can take easy till storm
Passes; should people passive lie,
They sure would get frozen to die.

Not planes, made are they for harsh land,
To nowhere wishing to migrate,
Paradise be 'pon earth, or Pearly Gate,
And harsher gets the life sturdier stand.

The poem dwells on life in Drass in Ladakh, India.

1. The pass: Zojilla

- Happenings | 14.09.12 |

When birds in distress call

Ironic it seems to me not the least,
Nor to those watching their withering worlds,
That few of them survive as in our midst,
More watchers wake up now O trailing birds.

If I the blue cap of the rock thrush miss,
Miss whistling calls of drongos[1] so pleasant,
Colours of parakeets, miss avian bliss,
The least I do: live up to lessons learnt.

The house sparrows— our all-season good friends,
E'er on a pair of busy brownish wings,
Oft daring too close to our sullied hands,
Have dwindled; but cell phone ever more rings.

And where has the pied bush-chat gone?
Perhaps Indian magpies and robins' way;
Cuckoos, sunbirds, thrushes sing all alone,
And seen are only on a lucky day.

Her haven on earth has when all but died,
Whence can the paradise fly-catcher come?
Easy though flies, their food, are still supplied,
Where can you find her fondest breakfast worm?

What else when pesticides kill aplenty?
We care when fewer green spaces to spare
In our blind zest for an exotic tree,
Few natives grow, nor for grown do we care.

Tall towers soar where fields were, meadows were,
And lakes if not levelled up are dug deep,
Shallow jheels² lifelines are for wings from air;
No wonder, whatso man sows would he reap.

Ironic may it sound, but be the least
To find a gang of crows ah chasing 'way
A large kite on wings, a bravest of beast,
And droves of dead-pan doves drooling all day—
The sole heritage we deserve to keep,
Not else but what we sow we reap.

---

1. Drongos: A local bird of the size of a bush thrush, greyish dark, with a tail like an inverted Y.

2. Jheels: In shallow lakes birds can fish for food.

-Happenings | 01.11.12 |

Lit-fests, pit-fests, spat-fests

Diwali dawns and noise soars at night,
Lit-fests too no more seem about light,
When cool controversy
Spells success, not courtesy,
Decibels do when dance to delight.

Last year, Jaipur Literary Festival was marred by ban on a well-known Indian writer living abroad. The recent Mumbai lit-fest was marred by spat between a theatre/film personality and another writer of Indian origin. Times of India, planning its own now, might perhaps be looking for a suitable controversy to ensure its success. Strange, but there's nothing like A Million Mutinies for success!

- Happenings | 05.11.12 |

If faiths can mature like wine

Fair if graves seem for them no fair sign,
Not if fair sex gets banned from a shrine;
I deem them liberal,
Their faith equal to all;
Here's hoping faiths mature like good wine.

Citing Islamic injunction against women visiting graves, seven Sufi shrines in Mumbai banned women from worshipping with any access to the sanctum. I thought Sufism was known for its openness and liberal views. Perhaps it still is. Perhaps they have a point that I can't see.

- Happenings | 06.11.12 |

Slap care

If you can a thousand dollars spare,
Beauty care now comes with a slap-care,
One precise slap on face,
But be-grudge no disgrace,
Thai thwacks lo, facial wrinkles to dare!

A Bangkok-born masseuse launched a unique beauty care technique in USA to tone up facial skin. A lady called Tata delivers precision slaps cum facial pinching using closely guarded Thai wisdom while assuring a wrinkle free firmed-up face. The treatment lasts six months. There is also a monthly package for US dollars 1000.

- Happenings | 09.11.12 |

The new India I never knew

I know not still; the picture seems cloudy
Like monsoon's pregnant sky, hopes still hazy,
But new India seems to me resurgent,
And vibrant, chaotic though confident,
As if her ancient spirit were reborn,
The grey seedling in a newly born corn!

A land, millions of starving mouths no more,
A billion hungry, burning fires' ashore;
Amid islands rich with wealth aplenty,
Mired in a sea of abject poverty,
Illiterate raw heads 'pon hungry maws,
A common caste cast in consumer cause.

The dreamers dreaming for a better life,
All watching winds of change on screens raised rife,
Hundreds of them in far-flung homes sans let,
Homes thatched, unmatched, but with an idiot set,
Connected, closeted by phone mobile,
Many now moved by an automobile.

Greed and growth grabbing wealth o'er flowing rims,
A pair of wings to nebulous their dreams,
Mixing odd potions, a heady cocktail
Across, of young minds on the move to hail
New India in an unforeseen hurry,
Wonder if old paradigm to burry.

Where's common man in this tectonic shift?
Where's pension pusher, one without? Adrift
In a daze, jostled for a mere toe-hold,
Hapless and mute, scrambling for life blind-fold,
O in a new nation of scams and scandals,
Lost in a storm and boats have shattered hulls.

Ways of my world have selfish grown, O Lord,
Bordering on white-collar theft and fraud:
A man is slain, but no'ne the butcher is,
A fraud's been fraught, at large fraudster in ease,
One plucks, a partner packs and profit makes,
Commits, confesses nor, but still partakes.

---

1. Burning fires: alludes to aspiring consumers.

The last stanza draws inspiration from the American philosopher, Ralph Waldo Wilson's 'The ways of trade and politics are grown selfish to the borders of theft . . . and fraud. The sins of our trade belong to no class, to no individual. One plucks, one distributes, one eats. Everybody partakes, everybody confesses . . . Yet none feels accountable, we are all implicated. He did not create the abuse; he cannot alter it . . .'

- Happenings | 03.01.11 |

Manhood and media space

'Tis passé 'pon prying eyes to pose nude,
But mankind's not reached height of ways crude,
Yet, isn't it down-right lewd
To get logo tattooed
On manhood? Or am I no-good prude?

A forty something German man won a prize of £ 20,000 worth a Mini Cooper for getting its brand logo tattooed on his penis in a live radio contest. Listeners heard him squealing as a female presenter looked on. There were many a crazy stunt, many a desperate act, many an actor contesting, and he won the car by a narrow margin. One would think, the man who won the prize must be an odd, crazy freak. But no, he was in good company!

- Happenings | 07.01.11 |

Health, should ye be such a beast!

Health has ways O to look to the east
When the west is what one can't resist,
And so I haply feast
On what I should the least;
Should ye be O health, such kill-joy beast?

- Tongue-in-cheek | 03.02.11 |

Tree born on border pillar

A row of border pillars looking keen,
White-washed, each bearing a number in black,
Like suture-marks on earth's unfolding skin,
Wound thro' forests, farms, 'pon a sandy track.

Yet pillars were, not placed there to unite
The land; dividing lives, raising red ripples,
Dissected land that was ere seamless one,
They clipped a common tongue that fused peoples.

A spot where once was not but a pillar,
A sprawling Peepal tree spreads wings in place,
A tree born off a single bird dropping;
Perhaps it could not stand stone's grassy grace!

Poor bird, born there or from across border,
Harvested, whose seeds it happened to eat?
No one could tell, nor did a soul e'er care,
But with disdain do birds all borders beat.

Nourished by wind-wafted soil the tree grew,
And grew, crushing stony pillar to dust
Man-made dividers giving in to life—
As if frowning foisted pegs as unjust.

No soldier that watched borders had the heart
The sapling to uproot, much less grown hunk;
None of the neighbours thought of replacing
The pillar; but scratched their thoughts on the trunk.

The Peepal tree flourished, the tree of life,
Which, scriptures[1] have commended, severed be;
And stony pillar post stood sacrificed,
The tree survived that taught them unity.

It stands now cooling borders on each side,
And tempers too that restless on sleeves dwell,
Teaching: trees unite what borders divide,
Which, aught be erased were peace to prevail.

And what the people failed, a small bird did,
For, winged feathers for no built-borders care;
The bird perhaps was sent by destiny
O to teach bleeding hearts: do learn to share.

Based on a report in News week— true happening on Indo-Pak border at Suchetgarh.

1.   In an allegoric reference to Peepal tree that represents a mundane world and its life (Bhagavad-Gita # 15.3).

- Happenings | 05.02.11 |

The secret of Mona Lisa

Enigmatic e'er since it began,
Yet, smile came from no lovely woman,
But off a model muse—
A male— as goes the news,
A slender, female-like facile man!

The secret of the enigmatic smile is out. An Italian art historian has claimed that the model used in Leonardo's master-piece was his male muse— a young, effeminate, slender man with long, auburn curls. They were probably lovers. It was a self portrait as earlier believed. The secret was revealed by high magnification technique which showed up an S, the first letter of the male muse's name. And I am tempted to say:

The smile enigmatic ere was,
The painter too now as his cause!

- Happenings | 06.02.11 |

The heart is when young

Worried, he too would bow to ripe old age,
Yayati[1] though was in his wrinkles wrung,
His passions and desire were still too young—
O how to breathe life to the old age rage.

Three sons, own blood, when shied from life to share,
Puru[2] parted a piece of precious life,
The old king now a newly sharpened knife,
He enjoyed life, no indulgence to spare.

This happened ages ere in ancient past,
When heeding to hungry loins was common
As heeding maws, sex lived not at half mast,
And scarce was hidden hind a sleeping sun.

He knew, desires live long and yon of grave,
Turn, nor return finding a fastened gate,
That passion suffers no expiry date,
Desires burn bright fuelled by faggots of crave.

And love being no youth monopoly,
Nor a Valentine Day a game of dart,
Matures love with age, no youthful folly,
Flesh hankers, but does heed the call of heart.

---

1. **Yayati**: As the epic goes, he lived thousands of years before the
   Mahabharata War. He wanted to live longer than his lifespan
   and enjoy pleasures of life and wished to borrow life from whoso

can give. On checking with his sons the elder three refused, but the youngest son, Puru[2], obliged.

2. **Puru**: Yayati's[1] youngest son. His father, the king, being pleased with him made him the heir of vast kingdom, which he extended to the east, north of India. He bequeathed his name to the family line known as Purus.

Written on the eve of Valentine's Day

- Happenings | 07.02.11 |

Boot polish, ego maalish

Leaving tell-tale marks gone has the crown,
Stamping boots, their ways at brown to frown,
But servile still polish,
Egoist minds maalish[1],
Bend backward and forward as oft down.

---

1. maalish: Hindi, meaning massage.

As the legend goes, Sir Walter Raleigh gallantly spread his cape over a puddle for Queen Elizabeth to cross. In India of today, his tribe has prospered and multiplied, proving that chivalry (read, servility) is far from dead. Take this personal security officer of UP Chief Minister, a stern woman. Seeing her soiled shoes, he whipped out kerchief polishing the dirt off. Snakes have long passed by, their body marks still remain. Sycophants are still prone to bend backward and down.

- Happenings | 08.02.11 |

Portable now spells everything

A thing that ere was there for sure
As death, and stuck for life is now
Portable; a promiscuous lure
That's incurable what so how.

Not just nameless numbers mobile,
Portable goes automobile,
Insurance numbers, ere an isle,
And be part of portable pile.

Man once mindful was to image.
Name, nor image, he's now to number,
And bears loads of digital luggage,
Ah like a porter loves to lumber!

Old fashioned, he devoted lived for life,
But now to a set of mute numbers,
As one feels stuck to un-portable wife,
To politicians and odd plumbers!

Royalty had had whatso wanted—
Oft loyalty of men bent head,
But it seems for long set adrift,
Yet, flotsams gather as they drift.

And we in this land live in hope,
On promises like carrots shown,
But a hangman's hope is last rope,
And for years we chew on same bone.

This piece when revisited in 2015, I added the last stanza. Mobile portability is there but in name. And for others is still talked about.

- Happenings, Tongue-in-cheek | 10.02.11 |

And the death lingers

In twisted frame the death lingers alive,
Pale, rotting teeth tucked in a sunken jaw,
Nails grown inward, crooked into clenched palms,
Death kept at bay by food forced on unwilling maw.

In hospital that can't be called a jail,
Incarcerated in hail all the same,
For close to forty years, e'er since that night,
When violated she was in inhuman shame.

As a metaphor to her much-mauled mind
Locked she's in an unlocked room sans sunlight,
And body no better than a shrunk brinjal,
Nay, vegetables scarce suffer such mental plight.

Freedom's what she's denied— a basic right,
Intruding tests to know her mental state,
Fair dignity in life—of whatso left,
And human touch till meets her destiny's last date.

A friend fighting for her freedom to die,
Challenging mighty Justice ensconced tall;
Define, Lords, what life is, what dignity,
And heavens, pray paint not her lifeline's wilted wall.

She'd like naught better than in peace to die—
And die ere more dignity is denied,
Far from inhospitable, pale prison,
But laid she's helpless, due liquid of life supplied.

211

If this no prison is, none indeed is;
One sentenced for life is sent for one score,
Her tormentor was jailed just for seven,
Punished more for no crime, let her breathe on new shore.

Sporting wisdom's white wigs, white dress, black robes,
And blind folded, justice hearken none well,
Not oft the fair lady finds eyes and ears,
And lost is in letters of law to ring our bell.

There are those that in mercy wish to die,
To wear new garments, start all o'er again,
Many resigned await ropes in long line,
Who too should die; pray, cut short that lingering pain!

She was a young nurse in Mumbai's KEM hospital. One night in 1974, she was brutalised by a sweeper in the hospital's bare basement and strangulated with a dog chain. Ever since she lives like a vegetable, artificially sustained by forced feeding hurtled down her unwilling throat. Her friend, a journalist, who has been fighting for her rights, brought her case to light. In defence she asked justice to define 'life of dignity', courts appointed a panel of doctors whose report being too technical, vague and verbose, the court had to ask for an intelligible version. But, we often lack the virtue of brevity, clarity, and time. And while the courts decide she has been suffering mutely. She needs closure of her case more than debate on euthanasia. Besides, death is a friend and a liberator especially when life protected is no more life.

This piece is set in iambic pentameter. The fourth line of each quatrain is two syllables longer (hexameter), echoing the underlying mood of the poem— lingering death.

'Tis Death that life is sweet

If man were to rewrite life's mortal code,
Conquering age, banishing for good, death,
To stand 'lone bearing life's back-breaking load,
Would life smile on him in such deathless faith?

Machines howso smart scarce can conscious be,
Myriads of mirrors in an infinite
Hall of heavens that each to each can see,
Radiating life in a darkling night!

But what dies is body with soul aware,
What gain in garnishing a garment old?
What gain in getting mileage from tired mould?
Soul straddles all 'lone immortal to share.

And what use adding years to life listless
If ye can't add life to years, add more cheers;
Ask Yayati[1] of old that borrowed years,
Know what Ashvatthama[2] has to confess.

I can foresee generations of weak,
Old people pushing years, praying for death,
Pleading for a new garment, fresher breath,
Or for euthanasia's last mercy prick!

Lust for life 'tis nor living a long length,
Nor living vampire's life of a vain man,

In seeking life's height does there lay man's strength,
Or life at any cost— worms in a can!

The Mother Earth, for long weakened in womb,
Bare can bear burden of a deathless strain,
Can man beat Time and Space to search spare room?
Not death, man must master immortal pain.

And he aught know: 'tis Death that life is sweet,
A true friend never is death his defeat!

A cover story in Time magazine predicts that combined advances in computer science, artificial intelligence (AI), genetics, and biotechnology may enable mankind in foreseeable future to banish death altogether, making man immortal. Reason: More breakthroughs in science and technology are now made in one hour— what was possible in hundred years a century ago. Well, we often cannot even predict what the monsoon, about to set in, would be like. But this apart, I feel there are more serious imponderables man must surmount if he were to keep death at bay. Besides, death is a boon, no bane; it is death that life is sweet.

Yayati[1]: An ancestor of the Mahabharata heroes who borrowed years of life from his youngest son to enjoy the life when old, but realised, the law of diminishing returns applies to all joys.

Ashvatthama[2]: The son of guru Drona who was consumed by the fire of revenge and killed sleeping warriors in cold blood. He was condemned, shorn of all his divine powers, to suffer a deathless life of thousands of years in utter plight.

- Happenings | 01.03.11 |

Sedition, a child born in doubt

I've never seen a word of greater clout,
Nor one, more passionate to creed a child,
Ah sedition, an offspring born in doubt—
No motherhood perhaps was more reviled.

And fruit of lust— born she was of a Greek
Descent called 'stasis' reeking of stalemate,
Strange, but the word reeks of 'revolt' if meek,
Confusion confounded 'tween mom and mate!

May be she had had a Latin descent,
'Seditio'— turning to self, to one's heart,
In tension to move farther, far apart,
A twain of moms each to each in dissent!

A fond child of her motherland, England,
Abandoned there, but fostered in this land.

The word sedition has currently occupied people's mind as never before thanks to some court cases. The law against sedition has a colonial legacy. The word itself has doubtful, or rather conflicting etymology. A democracy should have no place for sedition, as preservation and status quo are against the grain of the rule of people. In democracy, change should always be welcome.

This poem highlights the conflicting parentage of the word. The last two lines allude to the fact that Britain, where the law of sedition was first born, now after long vacillation, has repealed it altogether. So have many countries. India is still in two minds.

- Happenings | 04.03.11 |

215

In search of dignity

The Chair heard— horse as if trailing a cart,
Thought well and hard— yet with head more than heart,
Two hallowed heads leaned on legal edge,
And wisdom wilted against printed page.

The chair cherished the plea and not yet still:
We mind no mercy killing if passive,
Whilst frowning her unfair sibling— active,
Reserved right of the chair last word to deal.

Wise words oft walk slow, take time to arrive,
Fair words therefore are worth a goodly wait,
A tune many a white wig loves to strive,
And mercy's made to wait her date with fate!

But passive so cruel, cares no mercy,
And looks to me heartlessly inhumane,
It is active that allays undue pain;
Pity the chairs cannot quite that way see.

If murder in mind, red hands, were one caught,
Proved and punished, he might hanged be till dead,
Yet, this our legal revenge be red-hot,
But mercy killing's sin—murder in bed.

And look at words of wisdom from the Chair:
Her friend cannot closeness to victim claim,
What with but few visits, words howso fair;
Poor she! Made now to hold the cross called blame!

So, mercy has cried and crossed o'er the side
Where life just meant a bare breathing of breath,
No wonder life triumphed o'er saviour death,
And dignity in life has been denied.

Poor nurse condemned— to live barest of bone,
In a state short of life, short too of death,
And mercy much maligned, in twilight zone,
And while alive has died shorn of all faith.

The Supreme Court Bench deliberated on the petition (by a sympathetic heart— a girlfriend) for mercy killing of a nurse in Hospital, a victim wronged by a hospital hand. The much awaited verdict on euthanasia is now out: The court may allow passive killing, case by case; but active killing is a strict no, no. Yet to me active seems so much kind and humane to the patient while passive, torturing the patient slowly, seems somewhat cruel. So, in a petition of heart, head has triumphed. Life that is no life has triumphed over death. Dignity has died.

- Happenings | 06.03.11 |

The march of times

The sights came from Egyptian homes,
The sounds too were from native domes,
I heard echoes still from the past—
Of histories cast in recast,
Of victories by people led,
Of venal powers made and unmade,
Of Germanys, broken down wall,
Of Afro-Asian freedom call,
Of Martin King calling for peace,
Of Gandhi treading path of justice!

With their largely peaceful movement brave Egyptians, forced their autocratic president of four decades to quit. It reminded me of old echoes— this piece. But I only can hope, the spring rising elsewhere in the region is equally successful.

- Happenings | 07.03.11 |

The tale of limes

Merciless is mauled truth, made when meek,
The search seems when to hide, not to seek,
Truth when wails under veil—
And lies when freely sail,
In disgust does truth dare: how 'bout leak!

This is how the government works. In American system officials are grilled in public. But our bureaucrats, our elected representatives (look at PAC and JPC) work under a veil of secrecy. And no government wants to change it. Some right-to-information advocates argue that when Parliament allows media to access its proceedings, why should its committees work behind opaque walls? So, what happens then? Sweet nothing! Disgusted, the truth cries out helplessly, and there are motivated leaks galore.

- Happenings | 08.03.11 |

Weakness thine own sin

God struggled with man ere making woman,
Who we know scarce is made the way man is,
The same mould, same clay, yet no matching ease,
And harder did toil He perfecting pan.

Man's not from Mars, nor woman from Venus,
Truth is: no woman treated is at par,
She lives an also-ran, behind and far,
Venus seems man's whim, his pen's pointless fuss!

Or myth that long prevailed, prospered un-spelt,
For, women oft care for no straight logic,
To them it's heart whence hails every magic,
Quiet did women pay for how men felt.

In bearing man's seed no martyr her make,
If she raises brood it's her sole domain,
In motherhood no man has claimed his stake,
And price of privilege and power is pain.

And these seeds countless centuries ere sown
Showed reigning queens still, and Opra Winfrey,
As man is woman too may be power-prone,
To men mom and sis are fine, wife's no way!

She knows, a way out seldom is bra-burning,
Bushy armpits, hirsute flesh, nor pants sporting,
Haunting male nightmares, nor all this male bushing,
Bob-cut hair style, nor is it bobbitising.

So, march with men, chest drawn and upright head,
Hand in hand if need be, never behind,
Now in touch, knowing when to brace ahead,
And high time ye know which way wends the wind:

You'd better then beware the Martian Gang
That calls ye 'hard to hail'— her ears to earn,
Naming a dog that barks, bites— as to hang,
Of those that give but to get in return!

All ye need do is: stand tall for thine right,
From rooftops scarce to rant, itching for fight,
Nor prove thee better than the Martian men,
But put to practice thine rights best ye can.

Last thing ye do is: feel frustrate within,
Beware; feeling weak is thine own past sin.

A centenary of International Women's Day has little to show for
solid success. And in guilt I can't do much better than pen this piece.

- Happenings | 09.03.11 |

Love at first sight

We know there's love, nor light at first sight,
Hard job, he and she both to be right;
Jane breaks six hearts before,
Five times Joe is unsure;
To find love seems to fly unfair kite!

Love at first sight seems myth, we well know. But how hard it is finding Mr or Ms Right? A study reveals: An average Jane will have her heart broken five times, and is dumped four times before finding Mr Right. An average Joe has the failure rate of six before shooting right for Ms Right. But does it work well in the end? This limerick is not quite sure. It's like flying an unfair kite. One must first find a good kite, and then ensure that it is tied well.

- Happenings | 11.03.11 |

Relativity

On vacation, devoid of creature care,
Cool time in cold, in deprived scant,
Days in wild, a way unpleasant,
Returning home thence from earth bare;
Back amid plentiful to choose—
Simple cares abound and feel good;
Is it mood or my attitude?
It's like on luxurious a cruise,
But thank the trip that deprived be,
That days home seem vacation free.

It sounds laughable but this is what we often look for in a so-called vacation in the wild. We can't do without the creature comforts we generally have at home. This piece imagines what if we spend a few days in the lap of Nature deprived of the creature comforts.

- Tongue-in-cheek | 01.04.11 |

Beware, we are touchy

If they use a bomb and blasphemy,
We have a potent clause— infamy,
If rose by any name
Rose be, thorns too are same,
Call us by any name, we're touchy.

If Pakistan has her blasphemy laws, India falls no far behind. We have our laws of infamy. Anyone deemed to disrespect nation's sage, the father of nation, anyone on a pedestal, pays heavy price. And it is not what one writes or says, but what we deem to derive from what he says that matters in attracting legal provisions of this law. So beware; being touchy is our trademark! Many books have been banned, the last being Joseph Levyveld's Great Soul: Mahatma Gandhi It has run into a problem of this kind and the book banned in Gujarat. A reviewer claimed that Gandhi was 'bisexual' and was deeply in love with a Prussian architect, Hermann Kallenbach, Gandhi's friend and disciple. Truth may be otherwise. But by banning a book we only give dignity to a lie.

- Happenings | 02.04.11 |

Lal Ded

Lalleswari, what Hindus fondly said,
Or, Lalla yogini, somewhat loaded,
Lal 'arifa to followers of Mohammed;
A spectrum of all sheds dominated,
And endearings all if nigh promoted;
Yet, to honour this Kashmir's plural head,
In the face of hearts O motivated,
Inclined I am to call her just Lal Ded:
Grandmother Lal, and worthy womb, instead!

The 14th century Kashmiri mystique, Sufi poet, Lal Ded— she has been Kashmir's best known spiritual and literary figure venerated by Hindus as well as Muslims. But she has for long eluded claims of religious monopolists. Yet, since 1980s things have somewhat changed as contributed by militancy in the region. A book has been published by Penguin Classics, 'I, Lalla, The Poems of Lal Ded', translated by Ranjit Hoskote.

Lalla's poems are called vaakhs, derived from the Sanskrit **vāk** or **vā cha**, meaning speech or words (**vākya** meaning sentence).

This piece is penned in her honour.

- Happenings | 02.07.11 |

A lunch box that lost innocence

This vestige of the by-gone Raj era,
Alive still as Tamil land's Tiffin House,
A diurnal companion of many,
A to-and-fro bird now bears thankless grouse!

Once a blue Brit, now a brown-blooded word
Like many a colonial cousin,
Tiffin box, a fully subscribed lunch-speak,
Born a noun, now an adjective! What sin!

Modest, unifying stainless steel case—
A box— lid secured with straps either side,
And each compartment on its own beside,
That food remains fresh and flavours their face.

Comes when lunch time for myriads hungry maws,
Bringing to life land's every single shade,
Why, a whole spectrum of kaum[1], caste, and creed,
That bare of benign box no day's well-made.

But of late bearing a blood-seeking bomb,
This do-no-wrong dabba's[2] gone sinister,
Carried on cycles, scooters with aplomb,
A carrier be of waiting disaster!

What once a friend was to a starving maw,
Has been terror's foul face, unwitting friend,
And in disguise for deadly blasts, a foe,
A forget-me-not friend gone out of hand!

One, that came to town crested with a crown,
A fair adjective foxing as fair noun[3]!

---

1. Kaum[1] is Hindi for community.
2. Dabba[2] is Hindi for (tiffin) box.
3. The word came to Indian lexicon meaning food, snack, and hence was a noun. In Tamil Nadu this word is still used in that sense—'Madras Tiffin House; let us have tiffin.' But most elsewhere it is used as an adjective— tiffin box.

Wednesday last week, now known as 13/7, added one more ominous ring to its cousin 11/7 a few years back when explosives went off in seven local trains in Mumbai. The 26/11 is still fresh in our memory. A friend of millions, The Tiffin box has in this last case turned into an instrument of terror as in many previous cases. Terror has snatched many innocent things from life— even children of tender age that become live carriers. Alas, a plane Tiffin box has now lost her innocence for ever. Would it ever walk tall?

- Happenings | 08.07.11 |

The itch to ditch

The itch to ditch moves in reverse gears,
And has reached a cycle of two years,
If wed-locks vie with beers,
Too long may be two years,
And wedding oath open date, oh dears!

The law makers in Mexico are toying with the idea of passing a controversial legislation that puts a two-year expiry date on marriages. How should we in India react? We, with a rising divorce rate in our metros, where two out of five marriages fail, and elsewhere contract marriages are not unknown, the institution of marriage is perhaps crumbling fast; 'till death do us part' seems like anachronism, as live-in relationships are being accepted widely. But who am I to sit in judgment of what others do? For now, let me live with this Limerick.

- Happenings | 04.10.11 |

Ch-impressionist painter

A painter of class, monkey's no less,
A simian li'le master as I guess,
And looking rather cool—
From impressionist school;
What's modern art but monkey business?

Reports in media give a portrait of an artist as under:

A Capuchin monkey, a simian, is making poly chromatic waves as a painter enriching the primate sanctuary in Toronto where he lives. He uses his hands, feet, tail, and even posterior as creative tools. He has produced many abstract works selling for $300 apiece. The little master is named as 'Pockets Warhol' – his paintings impressionist (ch-impressionist?).

- Happenings | 04.12.11 |

Words Well Worth

Contents

Words well worth

It is generally believed that limericks are lewd tending to be ludicrous. If not, they are light verses of leg-pulling type and often masquerade good humour. While this may be true in most cases considering their origin, it need not be so. I have here attempted to lift the status of limericks somewhat. I feel they provide a compact structure to express a serious thought in a lighter tone.

In this collection I have tried them as verses that are thought provoking. Some of them are based on Sanskrit *Subhashita*s (Words well worth), but are not direct translations. The underlying tone is often humorous to bring home the point, but not always.

Tell no one how good ye are

Care no one to tell your qualities—
To learned nor to wise,
Nor to those otherwise;
The wise on his own knows whatso is,
A fool blinkers wears of his own bliss.

-Words well worth | 01.11.14 |

The only bird in hand

O to chase vain, mirages in sand,
Youth and wealth that never for long stand,
Sky-flowers all, a bit,
O like horns of rabbit,
But virtue, nor yet fame— birds in hand!

-Words well worth | 02.11.14 |

Ah to die duly done

Ah to die duly done, not in red,
To him dead, dying there's none ahead,
Worry, nor what has been,
For, morrow's not his scene,
Yet, who's not afraid— lay and learned?

-Words well worth | 03.11.14

When it comes to food and love

Well worth are words of wisdom of wise,
Troubled times winging ways when arise,
All us thought or two spare,
Follow the wisdom fair,
Yet, in food and love we wear disguise!

-Words well worth | 04.11.14 |

Ornaments galore

Charity if adorns fisted hands,
As does truth to voice sanctity lands,
Ornament if of ears
Be wisdom of the seers,
What use more to him that understands?

-Words well worth | 05.11.14 |

Friends all

What you know good friend be on travel,
As is wife in home and hearth you dwell,
When unwell, a good friend
Remedies be in hand,
And virtues, but when death rings doorbell!

-Words well worth | 06.11.14 |

The soul's on its own

On own self should soul rear karmic root,
On its own, good or bad, reap the fruit,
On its own aught roam rife,
One to another life,
Leave on sands of time foot-prints so mute.

-Words well worth | 07.11.14 |

Blinds all

A blind by birth cannot for sure see,
So is one purblind lost in lust be,
One blinkered by conceit
Can see, but won't one zit,
The man chasing self sees none any.

-Words well worth | 08.11.14 |

A monkey, and wears monster hat

A monkey, and gets drunk O like none,
And stings thence a mad, mad scorpion,
Enters soon a spirit,
Making worse bit by bit,
This or that— anything can happen.

-Words well worth | 09.11.14 |

What maketh it universe

Varied vie opinions pole to pole,
As varied waters are hole to hole,
Varied ways tribe to tribe,
As are views scribe to scribe,
Everything's diverse, but for one soul!

-Words well worth | 10.11.14 |

One blinded by lust

An owl can't much during daylight see,
Comes night and a crow no more can he,
Strange, but one must this trust:
One blinded by mad lust
In daylight nor yet at night can see.

-Words well worth | 11.11.14 |

Goat's nipples as if on neck

He that hath none these pursuits 'pon earth—
Pursuit of means, nor dharma,
Salvation, nor life's karma,
Vain, worthless nigh on earth be his birth,
Goat's nipples as if on neck— no worth!

-Words well worth | 12.11.14 |

Learned but him— doer of deeds

They that read, nor those help others read,
Nor those that letters of scriptures tread,
Addicts all them sure are,
Bookworms no less by far,
He's learned that doer is of deed.

-Words well worth | 13.11.14 |

The way to deal

Nobles by bowing, falling at feet,
The brave by dividing as to beat,
The base, vile and willing,
By petty things giving,
Near and dear by sweet words— but discrete.

-Words well worth | 14.11.14 |

Wishful thinking

If feelings felt on funeral course,
And those felt post love-making of course,
If for long should prevail,
And persist long to tail,
Who'd not feel freed from life's hackney horse?

-Words well worth | 15.11.14 |

Who can please these men?

Poor deer, damned they drink in their own den,
Retiring to far wood,
Browsing on grass no good,
Hunted down still in utter disdain;
None can please, placate nor wretched men!

-Words well worth | 16.11.14 |

Head and heart: no birds of feather

A good heart scarce has good head at crest,
Nor good head hast good heart,
Both by far way apart,
Rare is good medicine good in taste,
Rare it proves good in remedial test.

-Words well worth | 17.11.14 |

Leaves are of the same tree

Religions that claim to be rare trees,
Claiming unique to be,
Attract not but honey-loving bees,
Leaves they are of same tree,
Be-swept, be-nourished by the same breeze!

-Words well worth | 18.11.14 |

Strange, this poison pleases

Venom of the venomous varies,
Kills not ere consuming,
Venom of sensual cravings harries,
Kills but by coveting,
It is strange, the poison still pleases.

-Words well worth | 19.11.14 |

Good from far

Hills look good from afar,
So doth a distant star,
A plain Jane if dressed up and done is,
Battles from a safe distance may please,
Green looks greener from far.

-Words well worth | 20.11.14 |

No middle path here

The dull and deluded that not knows,
The enlightened that far ahead goes,
Both of them beget bliss,
Each happy with life his,
The man in-between wallows in woes.

-Words well worth | 21.11.14 |

Happy live, haply leave

Long as live haply live in heaven,
Beg, borrow, need be— steal,
Eating big, best of meal,
Burnt when gets the body, blood and bone,
What use worry, heaven or heathen?

-Words well worth | 22.11.14 |

Not what, how we see

One thing: three ways three sets of eyes see:
Mere flesh, an ascetic,
Beauty, a romantic,
Food for me to eat ah so fleshy,
Would be how sees a wolf so hungry.

-Words well worth | 23.11.14 |

Easy get, easy forget

Turns a low hanging fruit sour nigh soon,
No, none of the moons, we want blue moon,
Leaving their wedded wife,
Men chase other's all life,
Yet, coal be or diamond— both carbon!

-Words well worth | 24.11.14 |

Of virtue and without

Of men with and without fair virtue,
As is the wonted view,
Huge gulf gapes at the two:
Necklaces beauteous breasts beget,
Anklets fall further down, feet to get.

-Words well worth | 25.11.14 |

There is no man unfit

There's no sound that can't be a good chant,
Rare comes a herbal root cure that can't,
There's no man so unfit
To live and die in pit,
Rare is a man that can make a dent.

-Words well worth | 26.11.14 |

Mouths full, sweeter do drums sound

With mouth full, relishing goodly food,
Who would not in this world be subdued?
Paste dough— mouth and around,
Tuneful do the drums sound,
Sweeter sounds the sound of gratitude!

-Words well worth | 27.11.14 |

The meek, not mighty

Elephant, nor yet a hugely horse,
Nor ever fierce tiger of course;
A young goat would suffice
For divine sacrifice,
'Slaughter the meek', gods seem to endorse.

-Words well worth | 28.11.14 |

The seed and the sprout

The two words parroted I had ere,
When poor begged me petty alms to spare,
'I can't, can't, leave now, leave',
That this fate: 'give, please give'—
Haunts me, hungry hounds as if a hare!

-Words well worth | 29.11.14 |

Fame favours the fortunate

The moon shines with the same equal hue,
Month to month, phase to phase, both them two,
But one's be-known bright phase;
Strange seems fate's funny ways,
Fame seems to favour fortunate few.

-Words well worth | 30.11.14 |

The petty pretend more

The petty and worthless pretend more,
Lighter shed the clouds that louder roar,
Gold scarce can match the sound
That base metals resound,
Yet, gold's gold and brass is baser ore.

-Words well worth | 31.11.14 |

'We bow but to a rising sun

To flaring, flaming fire in forest,
Wind hails a helping hand,
But blows out a candle flame in haste;
The weak win o'er no friend,
The meek gets earth, nor yet land modest.

-Words well worth | 32.11.14 |

Fame to fortune's door arrives

Coveted was Kunti[1] by gods five,
Her daughter-in-law by hubbies five,
Both were held in rare hue
As women of virtue,
Ah, fame seems to favoured few arrive.

-Words well worth | 33.11.14 |

Death for sure

Wicked wife and a fraudulent friend,
Foul-mouthed maids flouting every command,
Night-halt in snake-filled house,
And snakes chasing no mouse,
Death for sure, doubt there is none at hand.

-Words well worth | 34.11.14 |

Friends or foes

Enough pain fighting foes,
Enough still, visiting friend when goes,
Givers both of grave grief,
And there seems no relief,
What difference 'tween the two? No one knows.

-Words well worth | 35.11.14 |

Men of moulds two

Men of moulds two malaise this strange world,
Both painful, hurting like two-edged sword:
A man with family,
Earning still none any;
Mendicant and still a mundane bird!

-Words well worth | 36.11.14 |

Tongue— a two-edged sword

Goddess of wealth dwells on tip of tongue,
The dear and near upon tongue are strung,
Tongues fetter, cause bondage,
There dwells death and damage,
Loose tongues lash— old or young.

-Words well worth | 37.11.14 |

I can't believe

A fool and counsellor all so sound,
Brave warrior— not a scratch nor yet wound,
A cheat and virtuous,
A mute and garrulous,
Credible is it, nor on firm ground!

-Words well worth | 38.11.14 |

Lost, if not given in grace

One wrong meal rakes up a day-long plight,
An ugly duck in bed roils whole night,
One prodigal son spoils
All of family toils,
That gets lost, given not with delight.

-Words well worth | 39.11.14 |

Half done is whole headache

Unmet debt, and left out un-frost fire,
Left alive enemy all so dire,
Trouble time and again,
And prove perennial pain,
What's half done fully arrive to ire.

-Words well worth | 40.11.14 |

Whatso is prayed for, pursued

Whatso one wishes from whatso shore,
Whatso goal, if prayed from deepest pore,
Pursued reverting not,
In part if not whole pot,
Sure he'd get— this man ever so sure.

-Words well worth | 41.11.14 |

What can be and not

O to know what not and what to tail:
What can't be would not be,
What can be might well be,
A cart can't upon water-ways rail,
Nor can a boat upon firm ground sail.

-Words well worth | 42.11.14 |

What's life if in freedom not lived?

A slave well knows: life is not lived well
Until lived in freedom, zest in spell;
Life breathing slavery,
Dependence-born worry,
Alive be or be dead, what avail?

-Words well worth | 43.11.14 |

A wise word from any a bird

Words that come even from a raw mind,
If reasoned well and right,
Let the wise welcome find;
Fine, sun's not there at night,
Is little lamp's light yon of reach quite?

-Words well worth | 44.11.14 |

The wise and otherwise

What lost is, beyond reach, duly dead,
Lament not the wise and the learned;
This sets the wise apart
From fools of head and heart;
Late in life dawns this truth unto head.

-Words well worth | 45.11.14 |

After grief and gall

Happiness, not so fragrant to smell,
But which on tough times tails,
Sweeter tastes, farther sails;
After awful taste, bitter as hell,
Even plain water casts tasty spell.

-Words well worth | 46.11.14 |

Nature or nurture

Progeny of a man of merits
Oft none of his merits inherits;
The ash of sandalwood
Has fragrance, nor its good,
Who does these credits, debits, audits?

-Words well worth | 47.11.14 |

Outgo peeping out of income

From hiding hole a well garnished grouse,
Outgo as if ahead
Of income— limited,
Peeping off from shrunken silken blouse,
Well-bestowed breasts from too small a house!

-Words well worth | 48.11.14 |

Words of wisdom to one no wise

Vain, vain does wend a well-spoken word,
If by an unenlightened man heard;
To blind that cannot see,
A woman's swell beauty,
Melody heard by a mute li'le nerd!

-Words well worth | 49.11.14 |

Love oft lies in loins

Only but him is pleasant, above
Else, in whom is found a life-long love
Scorched in youth's consumed fire,
He, whose loins never tire,
He, who need never his passion prove.

-Words well worth | 50.11.14 |

Whereon no alien hand moves

'Pon cobra, and miser's hoarded chest,
On lion's mane, on a chaste woman's breast,
On an eminent man,
No man's hands venture can,
Surrendered unless or on death rest!

-Words well worth | 51.11.14 |

In wrong hands

A coward as if armed abundant,
Knowledge to one far from confident,
An old man as on fire
In a bed of desire,
Consumed gets in no time sans content.

-Words well worth | 52.11.14 |

Empty vessels

Fully filled, a pot makes little sound,
Half empty nigh raucous is it found,
Man well-groomed, in knowledge,
Has conceit, nor vain edge,
He, shy of merit is chatter-bound.

-Words well worth | 53.11.14 |

Forget him or pain

If someone you love renders you pain,
This lesson of lifelong let explain:
If pain's prime forget him,
If he is, forget pain as bad dream,
Your love or else is vain.

-Words well worth | 54.11.14 |

Wait for no seventh wave

Every chance moment he did once crave,
But waited for so-called seventh wave,
Brave, nor bold, empty boast,
Thrown aside was to coast—
Memorial of his—a grave so grave!

-Words well worth | 55.11.14 |

Musings

Contents

A drone bee dreams

The lake's water be when lily clean,
And lotuses blossom when within,
I'd come winging, enjoy
With musical sweet din,
And it sure would make me mad with joy!

And how it unfolds

Night shall be over soon,
Dawn shall dawn, goes when Moon,
Sun shall rise, lotus shall smile again,
Oh thought I caught in petals, in pain,
And a trunk pulled it out in disdain.

Though anapaest is the metre used, the lines still do not follow the typical limerick pattern. The piece too shows irony, not humour—the first one how a drone bee dreams at a lily pond; the second, how things actually panned out. While it was lost dreaming the lotus folded up with the sun setting. Yet, instead of cutting through the petals, it decided not to harm them and wait till next morning, when with the sun rising lotus petals would open up. But alas, the second stanza tells us what happened.

-Musings | 11.12.14 |

Freedom

Freedom to think and act,
Freedom with all to interact,
Of body, mind, and intellect,
Not just from shackling chains,
From prison walls nor alien reins,
Nor slavery's numbing pains;
Yea, breaking from all constraints free
Be the freedom for me,
For which, on the way, up the hill,
And hope in heart we travel still.

-Musings | 14.12.14 |

Memories

An awful crowd in my solitude,
Memories rushing while I brood,
And touch me ere passing on like a girl in rush,
But soon to be flood, bank to bank,
And when I think of going across the bridge,
I find it far from easy,
The flood pushing me back,
And I never could quite know,
A crowd of one can be so overwhelming.
. . .   .
But now memories seem like
The ash on an unguent stick,
Essence eased out of the bottle,
But can it light up my lamp?
If so, can I fragrance get from such light?

- Musings | 04.09.14 |

Graves of past

Let resting ghosts buried be
In dark alleys of oblivion,
Of bitter taste in your opinion,
Your past is like a dead sea.
Why dig open the graves of past?
—Of painful memories lay,
Of a forgotten yesterday—
Not but grey shadows half mast
They'd cast upon a promising today;
Leave resting ghosts buried, let them decay.

———————————————————————————————

- Musings | 09.09.14 |

This humdrum human life

This humdrum human life,
Sun oftentimes as rain,
Autumn as oft as spring,
Pleasure with ever-present pain,
Happiness hailing strife,
One eye shedding endless tears,
Another fountain of cheers—
A warp and woof of light and shade,
'Pon life's canvas, delight and dread.
Man is in darkness caught
From one grey end to another,
Blind-folded be or not,
He's on a life's speed-breaker,
Day in and night without date,
A fig-leaf in front of fate!
Welcomed one moment, born red,
In time to go, done and dented,
Lost on the way and never found,
Keen he cuts life to come around.
Happenings all of humdrum rife
On an eternal tied-up string,
New, silver moon, autumn and spring,
This humdrum human life,
Celebrated still as it spells,
More in hope of heavens than hells!

- Musings | 10.09.14 |

How I wish they miss me

Bare one year to this day he'd died,
The emptiness, he not with us,
Seems to sound quite conspicuous,
May his legacy new pens guide;
The honest involvement he billed
A tall trademark be in this field.
Many a young pen that saw him,
And wonder-stuck in a fond dream,
Now meditate on his rare style—
He one alone stands like an isle.
We've seen him making the whole crowd
One with his poetry so proud,
Seen him elapsing in silence,
And struggling for words at once;
Seen him sealing his tall stature
In envelope, audience in rapture;
Today his fragrance is right here,
Gone has the flower that'd no peer.

. . . And how things are

One year has gone, more would abide,
His pen's silence few have much sighed,
Emptiness nor is there a void,
Many a new style's been alloyed,

The poetry field in this sense
Seems worse the least in his absence,
(As some would like to call
Never the verse at all);
He seemed a solitary isle,
Few missing his literary smile;
In his time he straddled the crowd,
His mouth no doubt a tad too loud;
No one flower has ruled the world,
Nor has a singing bird— my word.

A poet imagines how he would be remembered after his death; and then the reality dawns.

- Musings | 03.08.14 |

I recall

And I recall still all right
That silvery moonlight
When we first met that night,
Recall our love at first sight,
And super moon's soothing light
Has never 'gain been as bright;
I recall, now that we fight,
Moon's silver, love at first sight,
And everything of that night,
And wonder if things turn right
Again, rekindled as bright!
Be it a blue moon one night,
Or super moon, closer quite,
Had love at first-sight been right.

- Musings | 05.08.14 |

Poems of head, of heart

There's a poem hatching in heart,
Trying to surface, I try hard
Brick by painful brick, part by part,
My head as ever on the guard,
Trying to give the words new wings,
But child of labour hard if sings.

There's oft one regardless that flows,
Struggling though like Sufi sect.
As rhythm from depth ever grows,
The sound's born on the intersect,
And melody that comes to be,
The music be from depth of sea;
And when arrives safe on the shore,
Of head nor reason nor of rhyme,
More of rhythm, of divine time,
It comes from heart's deepest core.

- Musings | 08.08.14 |

Many a head, same Indian heart

If I'm an Indian, scarce I'd had a choice,
Yet having been one, sure adds to my joys,
Had the good lord asked me, I'd have opted
For a more affluent land, less crowded,
Less governed, garrulous less, less gloated,
Freer and open more, less bigoted;

And I can't say if proud I'm one to be:
I scarce can credit take for what went ere,
Nor am I proud of what's happening now;
And on balance, balance-sheet's far from fair,
Nor can else be— surviving on somehow—
A shaky ship mid-sea, moored on mercy.

No, I intend to settle not abroad,
And feel no less relaxed here in my home,
I may dislike many a thing nigh odd,
There's naught whatso still like under this dome,
This is where I was born, here I belong,
Here I intend to die singing this song.

There's something deep rooted in this my land,
There might soils be of shine, glitzy and grand,
Where for the head of mine may feel inclined,
So would my hungry maw; led by heart, yet,
In whatso way repaying my due debt,
To my dung-hill I hasten to rewind.

My prayer and belief, colour and creed,
Bye-products are of the same Indian breed,
And so I've Indian kinship no less still,
Religion and rearing notwithstanding,
And deep sense of brotherhood do I feel,
In melody my own the same song sing.

A quarrelling and cantankerous lot,
One might say, but that is the Indian pot,
A calamity might it often take
To unite us; yet, all bubbles' behind,
There flows what an Indian ocean does make,
Beneath myriads of heads and caps, one mind!

On 15th August, Independence Day

- Musings | 09.08.14 |

If only you can ever see

Naught whatso common you have with me?
A great deal, me love, if you so see.
What we both, as many, know as I,
In fair faith oft called no more than i,
In truth be square root of minus one,
Which, shorn of arithmetic passion,
To me an unreal grey thought is,
An idea borrowed smart on long lease!

We both, comes when our time
To go, in state sublime,
Decomposed mortal flesh,
To be a pile of ash,
Or be one with grave dust,
With all—raw feelings, passion and lust,
In time sub-atomic nought at all—
What once 'nothing common' ye did call!

And sooner comes when a moment nigh,
The mind does when with memories die,
Me and mine remaining though as ere,
The subtle, barest of causal bare,
Remains the radiant, all aware,
And rarest (if you may) of the rare!
There thou art me love the same as me,
But if in hope ye can that way see.

- Musings | 02.04.14 |

"The time is now"

Imagine on a lone, remote island,
Far, far, amid wilderness and nowhere,
A place no one ever set foot ere,
And there a ship-wracked man should land,

Washed ashore by the stormy tidal waves,
Injured, unconscious for unknown long;
Nature that sings along an endless song,
If it chooses to assail, also saves.

Oh, where am I? What time is it?
How long, my God! What day is it?
Ah time! One thing man may never beat,
From time and space there's escape, nor retreat.

Yet, lone islands have little use for time,
Time that has future, nor has past,
Nor has fair reason nor yet rhyme,
Days, nights resigned to live as cast.

And time, meaninglessness invented,
By, who else, but man ruled by mind,
Whose, true self, long buried half-dead,
Oft plays a feeblest of tune from behind.

Well, oaks and eagles were bemused
By the question on time that he did pose,
Time as a tool this land ne'er used,
The question, well, never arose.

But were they to respond somehow,
Land that lived moment to moment,
Present time that lone was present,
Would've said: what else, the time is now!

- Musings | 04.04.14 |

Let's cross the limits of pain

Let's learn limits of pain to cross
And walk across the greens of comforts lain,
Far away, tossing aside convention,
To kiss unknown acres of new terrain,
Pain is the way new things are learnt,
Curiosity may have her heaven killed,
And yet, without it Eve would have stayed stilled
At Eden Garden's confining— RIP,
Blissful, content, far from pregnant
With possibilities howso hellish,
So, let's tie unknown fears on a tight leash,
And desert ere it's time no sinking ship,
If not else but to see how frightful fright
Be, O give lifeboat to a safe shore a toss.

Let's at times seek no rescue flight
To see how well is lit our inner light,
And find comfort in darkling night.
And to see if our spotless soul comes clean,
It's all right at times to embrace some dirt,
And learn to live with stains on our own shirt;
Let's leave of absence to our old masks give,
Unconcerned if in open sin to live,
To let the world see the way we have been.
This is to learn crossing limits of pain,
Pleasures o'er pain have marred morality[1],
Pain it is that produces poetry.

Yet wait, this second thought,
It too sounds no less sane—
More so sprouting unsought:
The art of life it is avoiding pain[2].

---

1. Frederic Nietzsche from 'The Antichrist'
2. Thomas Jefferson, 1786

- Musings | 01.02.14 |

Give it the voice of a rainbow

Vivid, vast, vibrant be when dreams' canvas,
Potential though never be its cause,
Balmy breeze waft when softly ashore,
Come, I said, do open my heart's closed door.
It lasted no more than a mere moment,
And it vanished with all the gold once dreamt.
And remained scattered in its wake,
Drizzles of day-long tears that'd fill a lake;
The call of muted mourning heart,
Had no voice—yon violin's wailing start,
For, broken for long was tired string,
And nor it nor my heart could sing,
Both trying tired interventions though,
Nor music nor breeze thence on did flow.

You had the music once created,
You were the conductor that it led,
You had made its tuneful voice muted,
You give rainbow's range—violet to red.

- Musings | 06.02.14 |

This too shall sooner pass

As one old brownish yellow leaf
Fell, another followed and more.
The tree still shed no tears of grief,
Even as autumn came ashore,
It held her faith firm to heart's core,
So firm in spring was her belief;
In every green sprout, every leaf,
In every tender blade of grass
Was heard a throbbing life's still roar
That said: this too sooner shall pass!

- Musings | 13.04.13 |

In a journey nowhere to arrive

Let me live to be hundred and five,
O once more to be a child-like naïve,
And travel in dispassion
To reach no destination,
In a journey nowhere to arrive!

Though cast in a limerick format, anapaest and all, the underlying mood is serious. It is the goal, aim or ambition that takes one away from now and here. Living with no burden makes child a child. This piece goes on such a trip.

- Musings | 02.05.13 |

Fury a shy maid is

When angry I did feel and watched it,
My rage beat ah hasty a retreat;
A shy maid fury be in black mood,
And vulnerable nigh, vain and nude
Behind her gossamer gauze-like hood,
And exposed when loses she her wit.

- Musings | 03.05.13 |

The kiss

Lips, speaking a most unique tongue,
Whispered each to each into ears:
Let us forever remain young
In love— that moments melt into years!
Let's dive deep in each other's rivers,
Pilgrims we're at a confluence,
Both getting good, both good givers,
Let's live as one from now on hence,
Lips whispered in their unique tongue.

- Musings | 04.05.13 |

The winter when slumbers

The newly born dare leaving mother's lair,
The winter slumbers whilst in open air.
Bees when begin to stir, birds are on wing,
Butterflies dance, nature out everywhere,
Prepare their parents whilst making new pair,
Fledglings get busy thence O wing priming,

I 'lone in winter dream of a warm spring,
Alone an un-busy thing drowned in cares,
O building nor singing nor making pairs,
Nor witness to 'now' nesting everywhere.

- Musings | 06.09.13 |

The lost reverie

The receding night as grins when still grey,
Loosening her gripping night-long dark belt,
The frosty snow as mellows soon to melt,
As moon saunters to hide all thro the day,
The east as looks laced with limpid red,
The mist hind grey shadows begins to flee,
As dawn rises restful from flurried sea,
Ah, a fair maid musing from bridal bed,
As Arun's[1] bright amorous arrows aim
To ruffle facile feathers of the night,
To cast the reign of Sun's radiant light,
Day slowly moves in— rightful crown to claim.

I, robbed of an early dawn's dewy dream,
Recalling but nigh, yet no less unsure
Of its gossamer rainbow-like vague theme,
Wake; wondering how sleep is such a lure!

Arun[1] in Sanskrit is the name of Sun's charioteer. He declares the domain of dawn, arrival of a Sunny, day-long reign.

- Musings | 01.02.12 |

The graveyard of senses

A skull bowl and no more— was all he¹ had—
Ah one for food, water to drink, to clean.

And then he saw a man drinking— cupped hands,
Joyous, he jettisoned the cranium bowl:
My hands now can the touch of water feel—
The raw cool of water with Nature's warmth—
My joy now reaches peak never ere felt,
I drink no more— cherish Nature's free love.

What ignorant fool I was all these years—
Drinking water from a beggarly bowl!
Man's senses seem to have gone dull in years,
Tongue tasting food and yet relishing naught,
Music plays on, mind not in tune with ears,
And roses robbed of beauty in vague eyes.

And human mind made worse—gross to grotesque,
Things made mundane from what ere was so rare,
Like none-else blossoms each flower from bud,
Freshly chiselled anew without a peer
In all earth; for, it'd ne'er been, nor shall be,
And yet, it dies as just one more flower.

Oh passing thru life untouched by its bliss,
Man has a graveyard made of his senses,
The purest joy of seeing beauty rare
Doth exist not in world; oh what a waste!
And hungry maw wanting ever the more,
His wonder wearing with greed's each morsel.

Ah a fakir with naught else than skull bowl,
And today's man turned who's a greedy owl!

---

1. The Greek thinker Diogenes gave up everything and lived like a mendicant, naked and possession-less. He just had a skull bowl.

- Musings | 02.04.12 |

O thou river from heaven

Do think of thine divine birth heaven-born,
Think, who brought thou here whatsoever for,
Long unknown years ere, one historic morn,
A sage invoked thee when at ashram door.

And born were thou a river Kaushikee—
A family name of the fiery sage—
A sage of royal lineage known for rage;
But, tell me who called thee Vishvamitree?

Remember, born were thou to purify,
To make the place pleasant like paradise;
But what's become of thee I know naught nigh,
Revolting art thou to my nose and eyes.

I wonder if alive can one ye call,
Whatso flows scarce is water that once came,
And ye came to uplift, not from grace fall,
It's garbage what flows, shaming thine sure name.

I wish thou had gone, gone was when the sage
From the holy mother hills he did roam,
And he cherished thine celestial image,
But thine divine spirit now scarce seems home.

And spirit gone, left are thine flesh and bone,
Wherein shelters sullied silt of man's greed,
And lodged unto man's mind greed gets outgrown,
Polluting what is left of human creed.

I sympathise, what small rivers like thee
Can do when Ganges gets no fairer fate,
In silence she suffers dire destiny;
But how long— I shudder to guess a date.

A sage brought it from heaven for his hermitage and called it Kaushikee (Mahabharata), now known as Vishvamitree.

- Musings | 01.05.12 |

Life and Death

Flame flutters and tide wanes at life's late dusk,
Death drops shutters as life reaches nadir,
Resembling a lifeless stone in palm,
And a moonless midnight no stars can lit.

Life's throbbing breasts hide failing heart beneath,
As if to mask a universal truth,
And howso unpalatable to it—
That every life dies sooner or later.

And man returns carrying no suitcase,
He leaves amidst unfinished hopes in life,
As loveliest words may freeze ere spoken,
As liveliest poems may die un-penned,

As daunting sportive goals remain un-scored,
One-sided love gets lost to die wordless,
Waiting for another life-term, one more
Harmony, returns he to destined fate.

And death comes to dot two un-dotted times,
To bring together two random journeys,
Sepulchral silence whilst steels to pile up
Like dust on the legacy of lifetime.

Like kiddy paper boat life seems in stagnant
Puddle, e'er getting soaked, ever sinking,
A passing breath can when tilt it to drown,
Strange that it waits for a killer wave still.

And much maligned death, is no enemy
Of life, but on first-name term with many,
Lingering on still for eternity
To die no vain, but to bring in new life.

To death, morrow is a way weighty word
That hangs future on a tenuous thread,
And lives half-shut eyed capturing shadows
Of passing present locked in empty space.

Between the two there's but one thing common:
Life's lived in fear of death, death of unknown.

- Musings | 05.05.12 |

Lonely hearts

No Fathers' Day card e'er failed to arrive,
Nor yet a sterile call on Mothers' Day;
A family album on a lean day
Still kept deserted memories alive,
As did the once-in-a-blue-moon visit
That thinner waned as seasons changed unlit.

The Spartan place, once modestly crowded,
Looked more spacious now than it ever was,
A luxury nigh for an old couple;
But they knew, children had their life to live—
Life getting hectic, harder by the day,
Should not old bones happy feel to survive?

Happy for a few bread-crumbs to them thrown:
When do fledglings return to nestling homes?
Beasts are not known to care for old parents,
Nor do winged ones wish a returned favour;
And children take parental grace given,
Forgetting, they need cross the same desert.

But time has come that humans copy beasts
And birds, to let instincts have a free play,
Oblivious, human hearts sing a lone tune;
What good to be civil, to be social
That draws away man from where Nature is?
Love is not love wanting returned favour.

And still, an odd phone call far better was,
An occasional card, and a rare visit;
'Tis good to know they remember us still',
And better still to nurture a fond doubt
Than to stare at a stark, frustrating proof,
Is not it good to dream than to wake up?

So they lived, lived a lonely life at home,
O than be furniture in alien dome.

Written in blank verse on Fathers' Day (17th June)

–Musings | 02.06.12 |

I am happy as I'm

Haply playing flute on a river bank,
He hardly saw the king's men approaching,
Even when close they came and in a flank,
Too keen were to convey what said the king.

Patience in power seems too a thin virtue,
And good news from royalty scarce can wait,
The best from where perhaps comes with a date,
And eager they were king's word to issue:

How among fated few ye shall soon be!
Placed as the kingdom's minister in prime,
With royal honour, all regalia, we
For which have come; let's be there in good time.

He no emotion showed still, nor did he
Stop playing, nor was a tune off its time,
The flute floated as if waves upon sea,
The news repeated when, same was the rhyme.

While seated still on a small slab of stone,
The music getting over, he began
Feeding his fish with care motherly known,
Then said like a suddenly woke up man:

Do see that turtle in a shallow pit,
How happy he's dunk in a murky mud!
All joys seem his, worried he's not one bit,
Lost unto him, much like a chirping bird.

He ne'er tries to be he's not, nor to rise,
Nor be one up with rivals, nor does care.
But think of jewel-studded, golden tortoise
At royal court— for years it has been there.

You know, the king worships that mark of old.
Tell now this live turtle to come to court,
Tempt, you'd gild him with precious stones and gold,
That, king would bow to him as would all fort.

Tell me now, to what would he want to cling—
To get gilded in gold, or live as he's,
He'd rather be his own sovereign king,
Care free to roam, do what his heart pleases.

A turtle if knows as does every beast,
What's good for him, what's not, I too no less,
O to leap unto vile waters the least,
And barter bliss for royal strife and stress.

Look at the banks of these happy waters,
Look at the trees swaying in happy breeze,
Look at the fish and fauna, see otters,
Happy are they, happy others to please.

Harvest of the Late Season

The joys of gazing at them 'pon this stone,
Doubt I'd ever get on a royal chair—
The worthy disciple of Lao Tzu,
He was many years back China's Chwang Tzu.

He knew: power keen to grasp more, more to have,
Cries: give; give me more till it goes to grave;
And maddened by might, power always feels right,
Trusted the least, gaining girth loses height.

Power, unlike an early dawn's purest dew,
Extirpates man's every humane virtue[2];
For, God did say: Power or ye shall have joy,
Ah power and joy, each to each a tad coy.

Man's prone to pride atop a tall tower,
And more so still if chaired in Stately power;
Say thanks to king, I feel happy as am,
I know naught to do with royal emblem.

---

1. " . . . and that power, whether vested in many or a few, is ever grasping, and like the grave, cries 'Give, give!' – Abigail Adams
2. "Power gradually extirpates from the mind every human and gentle virtue." Edmund Burke (1756).
3. "You shall have joy, or you shall have power, said God; you shall not have both." – Ralph Waldo Emerson (1865)

- Musings | 02.07.12 |

Let me know where happiness lives

Let providence— if pleased— me bless,
And help me spot happiness,
Per chance flash a map— an image
Upon my life's remote blank page;
Let it explain from where to start,
How to proceed whence I depart,
The colour the place is painted,
And the door number intended.

Whereso the place be in the world,
High heavens, yon where stars are lit,
Open-eyed I'd rush rapid feet,
I may grow wings of a large bird.
And if not heaven the high seas,
I'll set sails, waiting for no breeze,
Let it be long nautical miles,
Sails, nor wings, leap isles to isles,
To spot the house of happiness,
Should providence be pleased to bless.

What length we all would want to go in search of happiness! The assumption is that happiness is far off and is not easy to reach. The essential nature of man is infinite bliss, *chit-ananda* as we call. All we have to do is dust our exterior, and happiness is there. Man is like a mirror that reflects happiness but for the fine dusty layer on the surface. And yet, we find it harder to search within. The result is: we look for it far in vain.

-Musings | 03.07.12 |

Footprints upon my sands

As man in poor image of God is made,
His footprints of acts scarce to my heart reach;
History may have recorded his work,
I need no such printed prints him to know.
I well can hear, and feel his steps 'pon me;
Let me wait till that wave rises from sea
Erasing wrinkles off my body's skin;
And if that tide, always a ready friend,
Whilst receding back to the heart of sea,
Were to take time my wrinkles to remove,
I understand; tides oft are tamed by time.
Let then a breeze come to my help as ere,
I need no footprints, nor read them to know
How he that just walked by on me be like.
And as I know, the sea by night gets tired
Untangling the wrinkles that the waves
Imprint upon my heart, as do the clouds,
Whilst fetching vapour from the sea, from air,
Returning as rain, seasons in and out,
He too erases my scars, there's no doubt.
And yet, I wait and wait— ah, love to wait
For years yon count for a rare man to come,
To walk upon my pulsating bosom,
To please my eager heart, to trace footprints
In sands of time that scarce can be erased.
Man sure is made in poor image of God,
That he evolves to bring that image closer

To His; till then, tides, help erase these prints,
Or else, O breeze, O rain, wait for no hints.
As you know, sands are grained from solid rock
O'er centuries; I'll wait setting my clock.

This poem, a song of the sea on sands, is set in blank verse, as the sands on sea that have seen man for millennia have a lot to say. This is what it feels.

- Musings | 05.07.12 |

Few things please us more than lies

Three scores and more, and I am still no wise
That few things please us more than shades of lies;
We lie to strangers, to those that are close,
We lie to Him that by name of God goes.

A poet's pen, portraying dapper dreams,
A painting brush creative nigh oft trims
The truth; perhaps, that's what art is about,
But I'd love to pretend I still have doubt.

We pay for a peep of pulpy films more,
For fictitious pen, as for painted lore,
We switch off news, opt for entertainment,
We like dreams more than minding this moment.

Most of us find the Fifty Shades of Grey
Exciting more than truth's bare, black and white;
Great actors get known by the roles they play;
Ah, blight of lies live longer than truth's light.

Yudhishthir lived his life truth to uphold,
Yet, we recall the sole lie he once told;
'Yea, my guru, Ashavatthama is slain',
O pointing to the pachyderm in vain[1]!

A cat loves none else than her own sweet self,
And more illusive is than fairy elf,
But still as pet we pamper her for long,
'Tis fib o'er fact here, right o'er-ruled by wrong!

More commerce is bought o'er the myth of lie,
More nations are friends, for, truths lowly lie,
More remain married for the same odd reason,
For, untruth blossoms whatso be the season.

'The cruellest lies are in silence said',
Robert Louis may have reason so to say,
But lies do get eloquent by the day,
It is the truth that suffers when muted.

And lo the truth, but half in odd measure,
Is treated today like a rare treasure,
And in a warm company of white lies,
Couched in courteous decorum, seems on rise.

Makes sense, why we admire liars that dare,
Detesting those that a bare truth declare,
'Tis lies that nations nix the path of war,
The suave subtle untruths are foes no more.

Sin hath many a tool taken on call,
And lie maketh a handle that fits all².
So, dare to lie; truth is no more in creed,
To stick to truth is to lose hard earned lead.

Harvest of the Late Season

Go ahead; telling truth any fool can,
One that manages untruth well makes today's man,
All others lugging hind are also-ran—
On a dunghill, crackling like lost hen.

'Tis old fashioned to think lies live no long,
But let us hope, lies would live to be old[3];
For, today's truth is: old age makes lies bold;
Grace be, at ripe age found I've my lost song.

---

1. Mahabharata, Drona Parva, 2. Sin has many tools, but a lie is the handle that fits them all. -Oliver Wendell Homes. 3. A lie never lives to be old. - Sophocles

---

- Musings | 06.07.12 |

To the Messenger of gods

Messenger[1] O of the nightly heavens,
Smallest of the eight siblings sired by Sun,
And chores so crucial, a small man must run,
Yet, slow down a li'le still, catch breath for once.

It was eight years ere I sent thee a mail,
And styled Messenger Probe[2], named after thee—
At speed of thine, perhaps, that of a snail—
It carried anxious queries from me.

But I'd love to send Rakhi[3] every year,
O smallest of my siblings to me dear,
But thine one year's bare my three months or near,
And 'tis thine hot temper[4], bro, I much fear.

Slow down O sprinter, what use so much haste?
Do calm down a bit, ye know haste is waste.

Addressed to planet Mercury, and meant for children, it sees Earth as the planet's sister, Venus one more among the eight.

1. Planet Mercury is called a Messenger of gods, perhaps due to its orbiting around the sun with a great speed. It takes just 87 Earth days to orbit around the sun, but as much as 59 days for one rotation on its axis.
2. In 2004, NASA launched Messenger Probe to reach Mercury in 2011, a snail's speed in planetary motion.

3.   Rakhi[3]: An Indian custom in which sisters tie a thread as a token of love for their brothers, who in turn promise to protect them all their life.

4.   The surface temperature of Mercury is +167^0 C.

- Musings | 02.08.12 |

To my sister Venus

O my sole sister[1] for thine beauty known,
Do open up thine veil of secrecy[3],
And nearest[2] ye touch my heart, ye lone,
I'd love to closer come, should ye scorch me[4]?

Perplexed though I'm by thine strangest of ways:
The way rotate ye —to us gears reverse[5],
The time ye take around Pa— but few days,
And thine day's longer made than year[6]—still worse!

I'd love to come and spend some time with thee,
But wonder, what I'd do with nights so long—
Is that the secret of thine beauty's song?
Yet, I must wait: what more[7] ye would tell me.

I doubt what my sons deem: men from Mars came,
But my daughters do love to share thy name.

---

1. Venus and Earth are viewed as sisters, Earth slightly elder.
2. Venus is closer to Earth than Mars. The average distance from Earth to Venus is 41,391,000 km. But that of Earth to Mars is 78, 340,000 km.
3. As the planet is covered with thick clouds of gas, its terrain remains largely unknown.
4. Average temperature on Venus is $+456.85^0$ C.
5. Venus rotates backwards from East to West so that the sun would appear to rise from the West and set in the East.

6. The time Venus takes for one rotation round its axis is 243 Earth days. For one orbit around the sun it takes less at 224 days. So, her year is shorter than the day!

7. In April 2006 the European Space Agency's Venus Express Spacecraft and Japan's Venus Climate Orbiter Planet-C were launched in 2010.

- Musings | 03.08.12 |

To my guru of great girth

O big brother, benevolent guru,
Keep shielding us from straying shooting stars—
Rebels renegade from the Land of Wars[1]—
My children do cherish thine brightest hue.

Bestow to us thine blessings auspicious,
Ye can hold ten hundred siblings my size,
Meteors mere mosquitoes, I surmise;
Thou art a fatherly figure to us.

Pray, what ye do with so many a moon?
Are not five dozens and more too many?
I wonder if you can spare me any,
Ah, just one for my moonless nights— your boon!

O tail wind to my children's curious wings.
Thou art a source of strength to all siblings.

---

1. Land of Wars: It is presumed that meteors are fragments of
   Mars, or a planet between Mars and Jupiter that broke up due
   to an unknown collision in the past.

- Musings | 04.08.12 |

Mars stands for no wars

My warrior bro, brooding blood-red as eyes,
My sons singing of Martian heritage,
And bleeding my bosom, vain boasts that rage,
Cut battle bravado down to thine size.

But I feel sure, 'tis soil that ye look red,
Born is war mongering off fear's false dread,
Ridding innards of all fear rids false fright,
And all aggression would take the first flight.

Inspire my sons Olympus[1] heights to reach,
O will them to visit, to verify,
'Tis native itch, waging wars ye ne'er preach,
Tell, Martian wars have been a wanton lie.

And tell them if ye can some life sustain,
Meanwhile I hope my hopes are not in vain.

---

1. Mt Olympus on Mars is a symbol of height, being many times taller than Earth's tallest peak, Mt Everest.

- Musings | 05.08.12 |

O Saturn of stern face

Hi there, my big brother of angry face,
My children seem scared of thine evil eye,
Perchance ill-advised of thine mystery,
Too far art thou from them for kindly grace.

I do marvel at thine rare starry strings,
At thine long, far too long solar innings,
But a few of siblings wear such bright rings,
And thine lore seems to soar on our mind's wings.

I can't but covet thine many-hued sky,
Which, ye two big brothers monopolise—
Ah, moons of many a splendour when rise,
Thine heaven might make the sun somewhat shy.

And thine son— giant Titan— we envy,
His airy belt size dwarfing Mercury!

This is the fifth and the last in the series of poems meant for children and addressed to solar planets.

- Musings | 06.08.12 |

Let me steal time

To re-live nor get life restarted,
Nor make new beginnings once thwarted,
Nor yet to time-travel,
But, live backward at will,
I'd like O time to steal once wasted,
To be in the race still,
To serve me a new deal,
O hoping to get served ace of spade!

A limerick one and a half and wishful thinking for laugh!

- Musings | 10.08.12 |

Death when challenged life

And death once told a much defeated life:
Life's no life, lived as if on edge of knife,
Surfeit with struggles, soaked as if in strife,
Such a life is many a mute death rife.

Me death's purest death, unlike death-filled life,
And heard I've of man asking on deathbed,
Pray, tell me Death, how long ere I'm all dead?
Tired I'm of this daily dose— of death rife.

To him says death straightening up, stiff head,
Moments may when look like minutes so dread,
Minutes stretch and stretch into hours, instead,
Hours take when days, and days years thou art dead.

Remember, life's lived moment to moment,
And measured too in a moving moment,
Forget not: death alone is permanent,
I dwell in life from birth living dormant;

Freedom there's in life nor yet from death's pall,
Death changes bare but bricks of prison wall,
All quarrels 'tween life and death, big and small,
Seem settled, death when proves him far too tall.

Life's a small piece of graph and traced too blurred,
In my poem, said He, metered nor measured,
Begins its life like a fledgling young bird,
Death 'lone knows life's length, when end is unfurled.

Eons pass sans measure for endless time,
While no clocks tick, nor dare at hours to chime,
Rocks break down whilst time stands without a rhyme,
Grounds chunks to grains of sands, earth into lime.

While life seemed stuck with its poem's first spell,
Challenges death life to dare worst of hell,
Devouring time and space, causing ripple,
I'm all commanding Death, male principle[1].

---

1. Male principle: *Purusha,* soul, the male principle, vis-à-vis life, which in Sanskrit is *Prakriti, nature.*

- Musings | 12.08.12 |

313

A window of view

I looked at one of Nature's wonders
Enquiring about the flower,
'Lily', said one of the gardeners,
Looking at my pointed finger,
Precise, to the point, and perfect,
He'd said in a matter of fact.

Not quite content, a man of science—
Of flowers and flora, all progeny,
Which, at school we called Botany—
Said, enlightening my ignorance,
Of Hexandria monogymia genus,
Ah brilliant but what a fuss!

Oh what a beauty the flower be,
My lost dreams' serendipity,
Of thousand petals all so bright,
A mystery of Nature's splendour,
That opens up dark is when night,
And closes 'gain in morning hour.

And that was when I this knew
That came like early dawn's dew,
Poets oft tell you nothing new,
But have a new window of view
That looks not with eyes—with their heart,
And head paints a primitive art.

To some he makes too much of fuss,
Not apart from genus of that genius,
To some same are lily-lotus,
Which, charm the same still to most us,
And called by any a name,
Their beauty would spell the same.

-Musings | 06.09.12 |

My wish when died once again

My wish when died once again,
As was its wont, an old habit—
When I failed to be friends with it,
Nor curb, curtail, nor e'er restrain,
It took my sole, my soul with it,
And temptingly said: let's meet 'gain!

- Musings | 07.09.12 |

The acres of thought

My acres of much-ploughed thought-fields,
 Their recall taking long, some lost
In memory at crushing cost,
And lost be their much-laboured yields.

But I doubt; what has been a thought,
Contemplated in form and face,
And chewed and re-chewed for long, aught
Remain un-lost in time and space.

If to think is to be alive,
Let me keep cultivating my thoughts still—
Be they lofty, mundane or naïve—
If for not else, ah utter mental thrill!

I doubt the doubter that I am:
Man recoils from labour of mind;
So then let me be amid them
That, in thoughts live, in thoughts abide.

He that seeds thoughts through depths of night,
And waits endless hours watering,
May by dawn get beckoning light
Which, brighter gets— noon approaching.

In hope I carry on to plough
Unknown acres, and not in vain,
To whose green wilderness I bow;
I know he that thinks as well can.

And I hope still, what look mere weeds
Today, would yield bounties one day,
Soon to become much valued seeds;
Weeds are greens whose value's still grey.

What if these acres at my shore
Defy as of now fair mapping,
Far from futile would come to fore,
And would one day begin to sing.

And when thinking on weeds a while,
Thoughts as if lost in unknown file,
And making last terminal mile,
Ah showered me this light with smile:

Man, by far of matter is made,
But his spirit rules stronger still,
The greats strong might be made in head,
Greater are them with spirit's will.

So, let me not let someone build
A toll gate 'pon my mental field,
The lost acres are to me dear,
Let them take time to yield—many a year.

In hope of yield at future date,
Prepared I'm for long time to wait.

This poem might remind the readers of Robert Graves' 'Lost Acres', reading which a question that occurred to me was: 'Are these acres truly lost?' And this poem was born.

- Musings | 15.09.12 |

Life a short span betwixt two deaths

A king once dreamt a pre-dawn weird dream—
A stern notice oh from the Lord of Death:
By setting sun shall I catch you, your life;
Dawn's half dreams come true, thought he waking up.

Shattered, he delved for long: how to beat death,
And unsure how, summoned his minister;
'The sole escape: beat a hasty retreat
'From Death on wings of a flying stallion,
'Leave Death behind trailing too far and tired,
'Beat setting sun, let no one overtake.'

Somewhat assuaged he thanked his wise vazeer;
What strange things people do to escape death!
Which, but tax is— tithe to take new veneer,
New garments as Hindu scriptures do say,
But we do strange things to evade tithe too,
Kings and commoners alike act this way.

Taking a wind-storm of a horse he left
Racing, feeling fatigue, hunger nor thirst,
Yon of his land's border in balmy woods,
Dripping wet with sweat, horse foaming in mouth;
The sun at the nadir but not yet set.
Triumphant at last, he reined in his horse
Under a huge banyan tree, catching breath,
Hoping for him and horse heaven's-hailed rest,
Patting its back, grateful hand on its head,

'Bravo my boy, ah, we've beaten them both—
'Death and Time both—and more, ah, saved my life,
'I care for none, Time nor yet evil Death,
'The twain must have been shaken in their faith.'

'Not yet', he felt a heavy hand on back,
'Not shaken in faith, worried sure I was
'If you would reach here ere the day dies out,
'But your horse sure deserves richest of praise,
'It brought you to Death to die destined death.
'This early dawn I was well nigh worried,
'If you could reach the destined place of death,
'The reason I had to be in your dream.
'Death does not come to man, time is when right,
'It's man that comes, O drawn by destiny.'

Just as a new dawn dawns like a fresh spring,
Old age and death are writ large by unknown pen,
Just as the life gets spent manoeuvring—
An escapade as if of life in vain!

To escape from inevitable death,
Some seek wealth and some health, some name and fame,
But time and death triumph o'er all the same,
And wiped out like footprints on sands of time,

Come dusk and tide, naught is saved to rhyme,
Book of eternity, a print-less page,
And carries to the end a blank image,
For, Death from all things born draws equal faith.

The church bells toll; ask not for whom and why,
They toll for everyone, now or near nigh,
And what is Death but a whim of one's mind?
Life lives betwixt of two deaths: fore and hind.

This story of escape from death is unfolded in blank verse. The poem is loosely metered in iambic pentameter. Towards the end depicting the truth of death, the poem shifts to rhymed lines. Perhaps, the truth of death at last begins to rhyme!

- Musings | 02.10.12 |

The room was filled with gloom

The room was filled with facile gloom,
Though potted plants filled the within,
And all else seemed incidental,
Contrasting with dullness without,
E'en at the peak of monsoon month;
Life oft looks incompatible,
Matching no man's fanciful whims,
Whilst world weirder is than we think;
The tree in front of my window,
With more yellowed brown leaves than green,
Somehow more reassuring seemed
Than roses pink with life in room;
In kitchen, the cooker's protests
Cried hoarse with rising stove-flame,
Somewhat spiteful of dullness within;
I wonder if man's best behaviour
Can ever match Nature's endeavour
To rise above defeatist thoughts of tomb,
Nor know if life's mysterious more,
Or if Nature seems wondrous more!

- Musings | 04.10.12 |

Death is life

Some live life chasing life in vain,
Worried, death comes when life gets tired,
Some in fear of death, some in pain,
Yet, all life, life in death is mired;
To some death is inauspicious,
There's naught to life still more precious.

Death a messenger if of Dharma[1],
In death there's no freedom of soul,
A parole, if not freedom sole,
It teaches to abide in karma,
Life's a lifetime of pravritti[2],
Death is moments of nivritti[3].

Time's when to go— body and mind,
To forget what we failed to do,
To leave all worries well behind,
It's no use 'pon spilt milk to rue,
But of the life awaiting yon,
It's death that takes us farther on.

And a fresh lease of life to mend
Broke fences of the life's farmland;
And what else there's but welcome death,
What use running away from friend
That fetched new beginning, no end,
O that soul can breathe in new breath.

This wisdom to me, no new bliss,
A simple truth I knew was this:
In all life, of mundane things rife,
I knew none whatso about life—
Nor knew, life's scarce life without cause—
O till death 'pon my death-bed was.

Dharma[1]: The Lord of Righteousness.

Pravritti[2]: activity, engaging in mundane things.

Nivritti[3]: karma-less-ness, retirement.

Most of us have most of the wisdom on life and death. But we have no use for this wisdom till it is time to die.

- Musings | 04.12 12 |

My mind is a wild wood

Pray, my thoughts seem to rush in flood,
I've everything but peace of mind;
No, my son, you wind and rewind,
Go yon, when blossom's still a bud.

I scarce know when, how thoughts are born,
And they are flowers, scarce young buds,
Fields watered, weeded invite birds,
Which come, O to feast on wild corn.

None can blossoms in their buds nip,
I am the crop, the crop is mine,
What hijacks thoughts can cut nor clip,
And thoughts are born living lives nine.

And when I reap what ere was thought,
A flower has blossomed from bud,
Full flower 'pon my hapless lot,
A water lily amid mud!

And my mind's manicured garden
Seems to o'er grow into wild wood;
Buried in hard I see the sun,
It grows wilder still whilst I brood.

I can't search peace though peace is nigh,
Nor can that hijacked, restless I;
Thou art silence between thoughts dwells,
Not wild lily that divine spells.

O give your thoughts no fertile ground,
Nor water; keep weeds within bound.

Wild crops[1] refer to unwanted thoughts. The poem is set in the form of doubts by the disciple and thoughtful lights thrown in by the Guru.

- Musings | 04.01.11 |

The mind a dancer is on stage

I see my mind as if a vast seaside,
And thoughts arise therein like waxing tide,
I see them oft meekly fading away
O like a tide waning with dying day.

And what survives is purest of silence,
Like a rain-washed shore in deep penitence,
Or like an empty stage flooded with light,
The dancer left leaving delight filled blight!

If mind a dancer is upon life stage,
And I but a witness, a silent sage,
Left lone on a rain-washed shore in silence,
What use being in idle penitence?

And if body-mind a vehicle in use,
O to be one not in command nor cues,
To see seas roaring, tempers alkaline,
And warning waters— dare ye cross the line.

- Musings | 05.01.11 |

I am silent awareness

I think and so am I,
An ancient thinker said nigh;
As a thought may arise,
Sooner as well it dies;
Ere my thought rose I was silence,
Soon as it dies I'd still be silence;
I was silence before,
I still am here to fore;
In ocean called Eternity,
Thought is a dot e'er so tiny;
I'm never I for my thought,
I'm I thanks my silence;
Yet, thoughts do never cease,
Though silence eternal awareness is.

Mind muddled with stray thoughts may stink,
I wonder I'm because I think.

- Musings | 06.01.11 |

Hope, a bird wordless that sings

Despair, first rain on dusty countryside,
Whose waters find no pathways traversed ere,
And hope comes like the next shower to guide,
O helping, hinting as to how and where.

With hope in heart do people walk long miles,
And a way ah from nowhere appears—
And from thickly wooded unknown hope smiles,
A thicket clears and a path haply veers.

And like a migrating bird on fair wings,
Hope, seems to come ah from nowhere to call,
Singing silent songs of eternal springs:
O worry not my ward, far off still's fall.

In hope does man cast his life's every wish,
Who born was with, a begging bawl alive,
A poor fisherman hoping to catch fish,
In hope would he continue to arrive.

And those I think that in fear would hope not,
O tying up their minds in tighter ropes,
I wonder whence would come a hopeful thought,
Whence would fount hope we call yon of all hopes?

It's hope that life survives all strife,
Hope is another name for life.

- Musings | 02.02.11

Hope lives on peaks and vales

As caveman, bordered men on the crudest,
Before civil were made, a bit modest,
And in a painstaking long march indeed,
Of civilising seed, evolving creed,
That had to struggle hard ere succeeding,
Many a weed losing ere mutating,
In a chaos that created new ways,
O from forests of dark alleys of maze.

Yet, there is no progress that won't plateau,
When heart vacillates— woods of go no-go,
And what for long years progress was,
Loses out on some strange new cause
That breaks every cause-effect chain,
Creation's womb bearing no new birth pain,
And mountain peaks begin to seek new vales,
And downhill do wend all new dales.

Hopes it seems approaches when highest peak,
The vales beyond begin to look nigh bleak!

Heart it seems lives on the edge of hope; but being essentially a brooding mind, it often delves into low depths, meandering, groping for a way out. Seeing the way much of the world is moving today, I also can't help but indulge in melancholic thoughts. Has man lost on a cause to evolve into a higher being? I don't know but hope not. Yet, civilisation, I suspect, is a bell-shaped curve.

- Musings | 04.02.11 |

Deserts, no less than woods

O to live least some life in dry desert
Lands— an anvil to tame man's attitudes,
And no less tough a teacher than green woods—
And a new man to be when we revert.

Men of world when tire, retire to forest;
They may as well in deserts choose to live,
In Nature's lap man's more of heaven's guest,
In solitude he His blessings receive.

Forests wooded are with greens and wild life,
Birds and beasts, butterflies and beetles rife,
Aloud they lessons of life to men preach,
But silent does a desert to him teach.

I doubt, God made this sandy barren sea
To induce from man a belated smile—
On spotting a solitary palm tree,
That he makes from dry nothingness green isle.

And if in wet woods there's a silver line,
Dry deserts shower a golden sunshine.

A few years back I spent late evenings in deserts of Rajasthan, where solitude reigns as in forests. But the solitude of deserts is a way apart. This poem reiterates how.

- Musings | 09.02.11 |

Man lone seems to lose faith

As drops and trickles from the face of sea
Evaporate and rise— rain clouds to be,
To get reborn as rain, and drops again—
A few of them falling upon same sea,
Some in vales, some on hilltops, and to drain
Down as rivers, streams, rivulets to be,
And some getting smothered by hungry dust,
A moment's life on earth— soon as born, bust!

A bird's dropping drops amid dust on earth,
And a seed therein begins to give birth,
Soon to sprout to become a young sapling,
In time to be a plant, a tree, wide girth,
Towering above all, tall and sprawling,
To sing in spring life songs fructifying,
And bearing a ripe seed in a long chain,
O happy to sprout time and time again.

And a soul traces much the same voyage,
Endless from birth to birth, and death to death,
And moving on to take a fresh new breath,
To rise, evolve to be of pure image;
Quiet does a rain drop evaporate,
Quiet does Nature newer things create,
But he cries breathing first breath, cries on death,
Wonder why man alone seems to lose faith!

- Musings | 12.02.11 |

Not Buddha, Aniruddha

When I die, at the gate of gods as wait,
Fains should He ask: why I lived not like Him,
Christ nor Gandhi, nor like any a great;
But rather, 'Have ye lived up to thine dream?'

There is none in this world made spot like me,
I my mission and goal in life to meet;
Inspired I be, but let me but me be,
Motivated ah not but me to beat.

Yet, taught are we to measure up to tall
In life, at schools to align with the class,
With footprints but mine I'm Peter nor Paul,
My own goals to set, tests my own to pass.

A man that lacks courage is scarce coward,
He's oft a man conforming to his ward;
No, let me not copy creeds of Buddha,
I'm here to be none but Aniruddha.

Born am I to fulfil but my own dream,
O to rise from depths of bottom like cream.

- Musings | 03.03.11 |

334

Smile the source of river called joy

I once felt from within a young boy,
Which, my heart translated as new joy,
To my eyes a source was for my smile,
That I saved safe in a well-marked file,
To bring forth when the spring of joy dried
For reasons that all logic defied,
But when I traced that smile
From my mind's reserved file,
The access was denied,
Under some rules applied,
The smile was why I felt like a boy,
Smile the source of the river called joy.

A merry heart doeth good like medicine—

- Bible proverb b 17.22

Set in anapaest metre.

- Musings | 10.03.11 |

Words and vibrations

Pyramids built human spirit to hail
Could not for senile centuries prevail;
Temples and cathedrals and domes we pray
In, tall minarets ere long did give way;
As would modern sky-kissers built to stay,
Bridges and dams, all would one day decay.

And so, I've long stood in childlike awe still
Of this great survival of human will,
That managed to preserve the Vedic words,
The human heritage that ere began
Close to the unknown history of man,
For, he sang in long human chain like birds.

Mere word of mouth from teacher to the taught,
From father to the son— as fresh, as hot,
Though tongues did change, religions came and went,
And wars were fought, lives lost since time's advent;
Oh, what a triumph of human spirit!
Of Vedic heritage, of divine writ!

When everything else failed,
The Vedic words prevailed.

Tomes of knowledge scarce survive on printed pages, nor ancient manuscripts can on hand-writ leaves, nor have words writ on stones and structures survived the scare of time. Never could the modern magnetic discs and tapes give us guarantee that the memories captured on them will for long prevail unharmed and un-erased by Nature's elements. Nothing can stand the will of Time, or Death in Indic philosophy. Against this backdrop, one cannot help wonder, the Vedic knowledge has largely survived.

- Musings | 05.04.11 |

Mercy killing, ethics or economics

My heart goes to souls silent in their strife,
To those in ailing beds, to wounded chins,
Linked to lifeless wires breathing borrowed life—
Which, try, be God from man-made mute machines!

Now in coma that were ere human still,
In care of friends and family that sought
To soothe them with love— the sick felt or not,
And yet those in care do the pain much feel.

Those in dead beds to nameless number turn
In treatment shops that seek somehow to earn,
Poor patients can know not they're yon of yon,
Nor do their loved ones know what's going on.

Intensive care oft means none's allowed in,
Wherein care concern is of mere machine
Breathing in breath, but breathing out life sane—
A concerned breast while preens through a glass pane.

Machines no more than beat robotic beats,
Some circulate blood, none them human treats,
Nurses come and go taking copious notes,
Doctors debate but know: bare sail the boats.

Intensive care may soon go extensive,
Expensive thence as measured by the bill,
While pockets pinch wounded go weary will,
To what end, no one knows till one last eve.

As oft does happen, ends the game one day,
Machines switched off and patients left to pray,
To fate when rests when medical mercy,
Poor patient well past untold agony!

Mercy killing no bird be of ethics,
It sings elegies on economics!

This is one more in the series on Euthanasia. The way mercy killing has to be undertaken, it has become a contradiction in terms. Very little mercy remains there. It may sound ethical for others, but for the close ones it boils down to sheer economics, hardly a legal subject!

-Musings | 06.04.11 |

In Zen

He stayed there for the sake,
When moved, moved in peace, love,
None noticing his move;
Serene he swam the lake,
A ripple nor yet shake;
So how he lived, left the world—
Much like a migrating bird
That in time returned from the lake.

This world's a wound and wen[1]
To some— painful tumour;
To him that lives in Zen,
Oh, what a blissful joy
To cherish and savour,
And left— a child his toy,
Time when to leave the world,
He who's a migrating bird!

Wen[1]: It has two archaic meanings. One, a tumour--like growth; two, Runic letter in Old English, later replaced by w, a variant wyn meaning joy (the word 'winsome' came from OE wynsum).

- Musings | 01.05.11

Who passeth there?

In infant dawn accosted sun
Arising from sleepy heaven
'Beware, who passeth there',
He just gave her a silent stare,
Quietly rising to be noon;
The dawn, now though a grown dame,
Persisted still when with the same
Query, the sun in distant horizon,
With a diminishing radiant stare
Paling further with the dusky air,
The grey lady persisting still
Though with her failing will,
Watched the sun disappear,
Now an old lady and dying,
The night, unmindful, rising
Phoenix like with her darkling gear,
Uttered, 'no one but Time',
Time passeth all the time,
All else trying to be in rhyme;
Time passeth relentless,
The world follows wordless,
And life blossoms with dawn,
And ages into day,
Unto dusk to give way,
And dies by night— day and dusk duly gone.

- Musings | 01.06.11

While lilacs wither

Lilacs when wither in hot sun,
When butterflies fail to flutter
In my ageing, unkempt garden,
Hope finds no fresh, fragrant flower.
I see a child in mother's lap,
Learning her voice and words with love,
Enjoying her aspic[1] nipples—
Joy that for long lingers on tongue,
Long after it loses all taste,
Her lisping lullaby too haunts,
Till late life that slowly withers.
And browning leaf in new childhood,
I unlearn what has for long stood,
O watching whilst lilacs wither.

Aspic[1]: savoury, sweet with love.

- Musings | 05.07.11 |

If you choose my poem to read

If you choose my poem to read,
Hold it not under a searching light,
Worse, under a prying microscope,
Nor press a keen, discreet ear to know
If her heart throbs and throbs right;
Let not your mind's curious mouse
Be let loose, probing a way out,
Let it not walk in poem's private rooms,
Nor look for non-existent nuances
Between two adjacent lines—
To see if there is a secret switch
To illuminate dark precincts;
Dig not too much between the lines
To search hard what is left unsaid;
Nor O readers try to hammer
It down, nor humiliate my piece—
A mother loves her child as is;
Pray, tie it not down, nor torture,
Nor analyse it into submission,
They're facts, figures nor statistics,
But a piece of personal art—
Product of heart more than of head,
A flying bird free to sing her song
That can be right, nor ever wrong;
Analysing it part by part,
You kill her delicate li'le heart.
So, be careful whenso you read,
Pray do to these dos and don'ts heed.

- Musings | 07.07.11 |

The grey routine

Morning: the same absorbed faces,
Talking and walking vapid walk,
Wearing shoes Velcro-ed sans laces,
Seen-before shirts, shorts, shades and stock,
Shedding sweat while footwear grimaces,
O talking same insipid talk.

Comes noon, lunch time has no new breeze,
Late noon, light's vigour beginning to fade,
Dogs stirring, stretching basked bodies,
Cool breeze comes, doldrums get late lease,
I brood o'er tea on re-tired last decade,
My tired bones welcome relaxed ease.

Evening: leisurely stroll nearby,
Errands on loose change bag in hand—
A day's supply of fruits to buy;
A thought, traffic taxing a sigh—
On grey life of bald head and bland,
Languid, listless, matching urban land!

Quiet supper of two ripe souls,
Reflect on life lean of new goals,
Book filled with yawns, news bulletin,
The day ending as began lean—
Of promise, dreams, lean of new roles,
And new dawn dawns, same tired routine.

- Musings | 09.07.11 |

Buttons I like, not fasteners

Fig leaf was all there was in times of yore,
Precarious, and held in place by hand
In Garden of Eden— an ancient lore,
Adam the sole other soul, a soul friend.

Years without count passed, came when grey raiment,
A sheet— to be wrapped much like a blanket,
And fashion was not yet a sole statement,
It was so for thousand moons, not a let.

All fastening was matter but of knots,
And life nigh simple, few knots, fewer ties,
A Spartan life free from clutters and clots,
Necessities when but from bare did rise.

Life was trim fit, tailored to fit the size,
And tied on to contours thanks a few straps,
And fasteners took ages to arise,
And a sea change when came— from body wraps.

Long centuries passed ere the next change came,
Mankind being busy with survival,
And fashion still a shy and frugal dame,
But change a child is of time eternal.

Harvest of the Late Season

And man invented— what else, ah buttons—
To fasten garments at every odd place,
And soon there were buttons in tens of tonnes,
O of countless kinds, each with a new face.

This I'd think was the first fashion statement,
For, buttons could boast more than straps e'er did,
And free of malfunction at odd moment,
Ah buttons for every custom and creed.

Then came zip fasteners from luggage and
Accessories, invading man's trousers,
But buttons nigh like a long lost school friend—
Faithful— free were from glitches getting worse.

Fasteners to me look like windows tucked,
Secured sealed whence no fresh air enter can,
And flexible buttons never get stuck,
And buttons score like a faithful hand fan.

- Musings | 10.07.11 |

Pleased are we when it pours

The wombs of heaven impregnated are
When massive clouds seem like petals of a far star,
A maid, eyes black and mascara applied,
Her black costume by the rain gods espied,
Roaming in a darkling night glittering,
And glistening with the flash of lightning,
This when I see in the nightly sky,
(Or is it my mind excited nigh?)
A twain of brownish nipples in heaven,
As if on the bosom of a pregnant woman,
Ready to rain the elixir of life
Upon lips of her offspring, parched, in strife,
And then, lo, comes loose all the sky,
O pouring forth and no-more shy.

Sun's no harbinger of passing pleasure,
And rain never is pain— a rare treasure,
Let sun shine in those sun-starved shores,
We of parched lands pleased are when it pours.

Without the rain— friend be or foe,
Whence would come the rainbow?
Whence would the silver line,
Amid grey clouds benign?

The first stanza is tailored on what Kalidass said about rains in Meghdoot written in Sanskrit. We in this land of plenty of sun pleased are when it rains— more so when it pours. Rain truly is the elixir of life. It is only in the sun-starved lands where it rains all year around that poets sing the songs of sun.

- Musings | 01.08.11|

Her fond memories

I recall still the two large probing eyes
Upon a learned-looking oval face
That should never have looked at me the least,
Had she regarded well the solemn place—
The temple of learning stacked up with tomes,
Wherein two eyes pretending whilst to read,
With other hallowed heads save hers engrossed,
Now stray, now read, return again the lead.

No doubt, she should never have looked at me
The way she did, who must have seen a few
More moons than me— the moon that while waxing
And waning in phases becomes the new—
Had she meant that alien eyes should not stare;
And it was how she looked that did me in,
Face nor figure, it was look in the eyes,
As eager heart tries to speak through eyes keen.

That, eyes chose to meet mine amongst many,
I'd still forget it as a random chance,
It might perhaps my spirit's weakness be,
Or destiny's well-determined a dance,
May be I was upon that lonely shore
Just when the pearl-laden boat landed there,
Strayed to my shore—an act of aimless oar,
No one would know; no one would ever care.

She came to my heart as comes harvest moon,
The weary year when comes to dying end,
And we could hardly steal many a glance,
Much less could see the destiny's gloved hand.
Were it random, it still had sunk enough,
God alone knows, moments melted alive,
My soul's weakened spirit fair witness was,
The hour of my defeat did when arrive.

Perhaps a false hope was still hanging on
A tenuous thread weak as was slender,
And I began to think of a right way
And wrong, I left my heart's mind to ponder.
I wondered still, was it her heart's triumph
Or my undoing, an utter ship-wrack
Upon my life's barren desperate shore;
And hoped happy moments might still come back.

And flashes of that fond love often pass
By in many a morning's lucid dream,
Radiant flames of my heart's young desire
Leap, only to become burnt ash and grim,
Whereby my piled up pride comes to perish,
Whereby swollen honours dash to dwindle,
And yet a vague hope still runs eternal,
That a dawn's dream may my heart rekindle.

I doubt still if she should have looked at all
At me with a pair of deep probing eyes,
Doubt, if she should have sought me, requesting
Me to drop her home, though what a surprise!
Or her pick-up car should have come at all,
Like an imprudent guest at an odd hour;

But now it feels as if it was long ere,
If it e'er happened; I can't discover.

The moments often fleet by in a click,
And my heart broods as if for long single,
In a world of 'what if' ere wisdom dawns,
And memories of college life mingle.
And I oft wonder why they weaken not
Like a magnetic tape, disc, record,
As memories as if on sands of time;
Perchance, some do touch our soul's deepest cord.

And our lives aught unfold as Destiny
Dances in a well-choreographed dance;
The director above, unseen decides,
And we actors know nothing in advance.
Man loses what he lived for all his life,
And eternally is designed to lose,
While at the same time counting his blessings,
Oh but from a given platter to choose.

And I count mine for these fond memories
Of her, for having gained her heart at all,
She might be brooding too to have lost me,
And here we are pulling our fate apart;
I, for catching her steal glances at me,
The way she did, and she the same way,
To pass our life's left-over remainder,
Hoping, in hereafter to have more say.

- Musings | 04.08.11 |

Fame

As proudest graves still get a coat of moss,
A poet's fame fades fainter like dull floss;
As greedy goats browse on tender green,
The under coat getting greyer and lean,
As head and footstones sink in, lost of prime,
As red brick-work blackens with time,
The seeds sown around as fail to flower,
And wanton weeds do above all tower;
The pages of his famous tomes
Now yellow, frail, and leave hoary homes
To get sold and recycled as waste,
Washed clean of all lyrical words—
Much like returning migrating birds—
To get melted in pulpy paste,
Once more to be a blank paper again,
And sing a new song, another refrain;
As grey lichens rule o'er tomb-stone's nameplate,
The crisp name and date to obliterate,
The best of names die with last flame,
Returns as life to dust the same!

- Musings | 09.08.11 |

Two hearts when beat as one . . .

Along a sleepy street as if in penance,
Swept clean, bathed fresh from a sharp shower,
The half moon hiding behind grey
Clouds, looking somewhat pale in dismay,
As was awashed old clock-tower,
Like a sinful soul cleansed in repentance.

The man on furlough now walking to run,
Till an open beach appears,
The smell of fish, sea-scented air,
A tap on window pane, a shy stare,
And four eyes when meet in long years,
The two hearts in tune beat as one.

. . . And then departs

The weary tales of a long wait
At once melted, as were all words
Of woe; in silence did the hearts whisper,
Now in years chanced to be together,
Lost in love's embrace— till the late birds
Came calling at the new dawning date.

And twilight hours more precious were,
Their love-lock more so still, as keen,
The long lost love now burning bright,
And beginning to be white light;
The morning never was felt so mean,
And parting, never so unfair!

The rhyme scheme has a mirror-image like symmetry—abccba— in all the four stanzas.

- Musings | 10.08.11 |

Canis Major, my seven sages

What all else doubtless deem a dog—
Four legs and a long wagging tail—
Ready a diurnal round to log,
As faithful dog should never fail
His master so firm, a Pole Star;
I see great guides, Seven Sages,
Who, having reached the Absolute,
Be around still O for ages,
To guide the earthlings staring mute,
Guiding the destinies from far;
While the Pole Star, Dhruva[1] we call,
A firm one though fainter and small,
Yet central still to starry cog,
Be it Canis Minor,
Or be Canis Major,
But seven sages, never dog!

Dhruva[1]: The firm, unmoving one

- Musings | 12.08.11 |

Missing you, O Nilgiri hills

Ah, to be at Nilgiri hills—
Now that sun's too much 'pon me here—
When his severe face he reveals,
Soon to be at peak in all year,
While shadowy hills and valleys
There at the Queen of Southern Peaks
No more drenched be with wet, wet leaks,
And dark clouds pour no wet rallies.

When April's marched, May when follows,
Black-throats when build nests at tea gardens,
Follows when a swarm of swallows,
Rain-softened earth when a tad hardens,
Flocks of new feathers not ere seen
Come, blossoms of spring to cherish,
Cuckoos, thrashes sing twice as keen,
The Nature then fulfils our wish.

To be at Nilgiris, amidst
Hills and dales looking damp, not dull,
Gossamer fog clears when, gone has mist,
Nature hast broken chilly lull,
And mornings wake not far too late,
And days when linger on long still,
To wear off waiting night-long chill,
O to welcome dawn at the gate.

Ah to be there amid new scene,
The hills when be a beauty queen.

Wellington of Nilgiri hills— I was there for nearly ten weeks when rains were at peak, and sun would show little for days and things would seem wet, damp and dull. Though the hills showed a different facet of their charm, time came when the sun was missed. This sentiment was reflected in my poem written during the stay. But, a weak monsoon elsewhere and strong sun soon reminded me of the hills again. Indeed, man always wants what is not.

- Musings | 13.08.11 |

Ye keep all the strings

Pray, preach me not from battlefront,
I know world's vain, nor life bad dream,
And soul's hunted nor is on hunt,
Life's still lived on heaven's sole whim.

If soul lives eternal, say you,
If death's no end, a goodly friend,
A gimmick to get garment new,
Man's left still to play given hand;

Play till death, life to life again,
Know not if Self to understand,
Life singing the same tired refrain,
He in new dress, born in new land!

Life meandering death to death
To repeat same mistakes at will,
To die slow death right from first breath,
Oh to get destiny's raw deal.

O teach me a way out from strife,
Your flute is a symbol of life,
And 'tis life you loved all along,
It's hard for me to see life's wrong.

Life and joys each to each well blend,
An if Liberation be bliss,
And world the other way should wend,
Then what use world, what use life is?

The world seems a field fraught with battle,
At best a shelter for odd night,
Never a life-long camp to settle,
Still, not rest battles he must fight.

Ye let man all the mistakes make,
Whilst keeping with you all the strings,
Ye let him eat and have the cake,
And ensure none can enjoy springs.

From one who has done a poetic translation of Bhagavad-Gita and still is left with nagging doubts, here is a tongue-in-cheek interpretation of the text.

- Musings | 14.08.11 |

Techno-inventions

Move over gadgets man can do without,
Give me this day devices not in doubt,
Like paper clips, tissues— user's staple,
Elastic bands, bubble-wraps so many,
Which, touch a billion lives of lay people,
And costing still less than precious penny;
Jewels of genius forever revered,
Workhorses like a light bulb so treasured;
Movers of the masses of any age,
More of a product packed, less a package.

But man also is green with greed within,
He does not always live by the bare need,
His heart envying neighbour's lawn so green,
Steve Jobs perhaps was first this to well read.

The world is into greed marketing from what was based on need. Apple's Steve Jobs (who dies on 5th Oct 2011) was among many that knew this well. But my mind goes to simple inventions that moved and maddened the world, rather those that cost a penny and still revolutionised the world.

- Musings | 03.10.11 |

Death, come; no time's too soon

Death, come; let far off be still mid-night's noon,
Thine fault I feel founts from waiting tad long,
Come at appointed time, thou art a boon,
To scorn thee is to let the life prolong;
Ye come to do thine job perfunctory,
'It's life that seems to me a mystery!

All men mortal are made right from first breath,
And life mere milestones in the path of death,
To all eventual ends, I believe,
Death seldom seems to me monstrous devil
It deems; where's death in life, life when we leave?
And soul that has its own will survives still.

Nor death to me is unresolved a riddle,
As life lives long— man still firm in the saddle,
Still finds evolution an unmixed struggle,
When ye call, I know better than to haggle!
If to die ere its time sin is evil,
To die not when time comes is greater still.

Winning, goal post but once is no life's aim
But tackling, till death brings in the lull,
To keep the ball in play till last whistle;
And still what ends is one round, not the game;
Remember, there always is extra time,
Should one have raw grit, the game and game's grime!

Aniruddha Pathak

So Death, do thine worst; sun that rises sets,
Spot on to plunge into my next voyage,
I'm penning my life's penultimate page,
To leap in dark ere it nigh frightful gets;
Here, warding winter like migrating birds,
I know no time to write my life's last words.

And when ye come at last, help me O Death,
With my baggage of babbles, my pen's crimes,
Oft whispering half truths writ in good faith,
That I can polish— paper, pen, new climes;
So let me die pen in hand, chosen post,
Till then, come to inspire me as thine host.

- Musings | 03.11.11 |

My epithets

Here was he set to flame, he the hash
Of a half-wit now done to grey ash,
Spare tears, spare weighty words,
He's gone go where all birds,
O deeds of thousand grey shades to cash.
. . .   .
Man is born to smoulder all his life—
Amid bliss, blessed joys, rife with strife,
Laid here to lose what left,
Deeds and naught, the old heft,
And whatso was spared by surgeon's knife*.

---

* I wish to donate my dead body— for whatever it is worth— for medical use.

Here was he laid to disintegrate
Unto Nature, such is destined date;
He died of every dent—
All thro life, each moment,
Shed no tears, shall be back soon than late!

- Musings | 06.11.11 |

Miscellany

Contents

A friend never seems far

To peacocks if hills are never far,
Nor ever rain-carrying clouds are,
To lilies white, if Sun is not far,
Which when arises all smile they are,
If to blue lilies Moon is the star,
And whoso be whose friend is not far,
Why man be from each to each afar,
Wonder why he lives like distant star.

This small introspective piece is set in anapaest metre.

-Reflections | 05.12.14 |

Mood mars as much as can

To him that chases mind his own,
No means are marked far too sacred,
He who's caught in Cupid's passion,
No signal cautions, none is red;
To him keen on knowledge and learning,
Comfort nor sleep nor needs seem prime;
To one intent on eating,
What good's relish, appetite, time?
Yet, keen to write to this my pen,
Ah even mood mars much as can!

-Tongue-in-cheek | 08.12.14 |

Politicians and priests

No angels both hate a happy world,
Both hungry hounds hunting hairs in herd,
Promising good morrows,
Wiping unheard sorrows,
Both end up souring today's fair curd.

Politicians and priests, ah what a tribe! They survive exploiting vested interests. Both need miserable men, not a happy world. A happy world would care little for them. A miserable man obeys, submits, and believes in what they promise. A happy man is not enamoured by promised paradise. But in countries kept poor the two Ps would prosper.

-Reflections | 12.12.14 |

If lost he has him

Place in sun, powered seat,
And world at his feet,
What good if lost he has him?

- Haikus | 06.08.14 |

A poem is pilgrimage

On a pilgrimage,
Faith in heart and pen,
And what guides is vague image.

- Haikus | 11.08.14 |

A poem is love

A vague thought in head,
And heart moves ahead,
And it goes on by love led.

- Haikus | 12.08.14 |

No struggle, no music

River in mood gay,
Not so blocks her way,
And there is music, nor play.

- Haikus | 13.08.14 |

If life is like a well

Life, thou art a well,
If I fill up ye won't spell,
And when I empty, ye swell.

- Haikus | 15.08.14 |

Thru wonder wends the way to God

Soon as the soft arrows
Of your early dawn,
There begins to play in each grain
Honey-filled music ever soothing;
O Grant to my small life
Content, nor quench worth a whit,
Let my eyes ever remain in thirst,
Let it fill an ocean of tears,
Whilst you reside in my mind,
And hiding my sorrows
I'd pretend searching you,
While getting to know your every grain—
What exists, what does not—
You remaining in my teary eyes,
Somewhat hazy and still clear enough,
That I see the world through you,
See thine world, though still not you.

Translated from the original in Hindi (Mahageeta, by Rajnish)

- Translations | 16.08.14 |

Death can conquer not,

Whatso gets green comes when spring,
By autumn grey sure shall gall,
To whatso born, and living,
Death shall doubtless one day call.

No happiness does feel shy
With so much death all around,
Man grieves and gathers up nigh,
Life survives holding her ground.

Amidst thorns still a pricking,
Flowers do keep blossoming,
Daily does death catch many,
Life lives, gives death no penny.

Look at miracle of life
Trapped in a sorrowful strife!
Death is in vain battle caught,
And life defeated is not.

Let autumn do her damnedest,
Spring shall spawn to do her best.

- Musings | 17.08.14 |

Trust and faith

Beware,
My voice once said:
Trust truth if proof is good,
Faith stands alone in solitude,
Eyes closed.

- Cinquains | 04.07.14 |

Go add to the beauty of life

No pilgrimage on a hired mule,
Nor yet so much a learning school,
Regulation nor is there rule,
No use treading way-trodden track,
Go discover— forward and back,
If enough love in life you pack,
Know this: life's a creative tool.

Go add to the beauty of life,
Banish as much you can its strife.
Add music, enhance melody,
Lift up its charming poetry,
And if you can, perchance,
Add a little more dance,
Life is creative tool, no chance.

This piece (a sort of sonnet) tells us what life is not, what it is, and what one should do.

- Musings | 08.07.14 |

Peak-less path up the hill

Should world a fitter place be to live,
And better gets by the passing day;
If we keep earning more, eat better,
Live haply much longer than before;
If rich gets richer, poor is pushed still,
If graph's grown faster for five decades—
Than in five hundred that preceded;
If healthy we grow and taller nigh,
And freer in all the history;
Consuming ever more calories,
Watts, horsepower, gigabytes and square feet,
Megahertz, air mileage, miles per lit;
If we get best of things from far shores,
And global trade gathers from all doors;
Luckiest lot ever born are we,
Freedom, peace, leisure time may it be,
Or learning, Medicare, travel clime,
Why's there grumbling and gloom, and such crime?

We prosper, pathetic the more get,
Invent more, enabled e'er more still,
What good be becoming better yet,
Where's the catch? Where's hidden the devil?

The progress the world has made is beyond doubt. Yet, there sure
something is amiss. In his book, The Rational Optimist, Matt
Ridley argues that the world has become a better place to live than
ever before. This piece (in anapaest metre) takes off from him.

- Reflections | 11.07.14 |

Travel

Travel,
Travel yet more,
Pilgrimage shore to shore,
In this life and yon; who can tell
Where to!

- Cinquains | 09.06.14 |

Know good-before date, O guest

He's the will, heart to serve, host is kind,
How long still O dear guest should you stay?
> *Honoured guest, your welcome is well-lined,*
> *Reason still is it to overstay?*
Time you know leaves things too stale behind,
So leave bags and baggage, why delay?
> *Good as God is the guest, host's faith blind,*
> *O let not his welcome still decay,*
Dateless[1] should all return, keep in mind,
Pray, taxing one's patience does not pay.
Taken care though, doted and well dined,
Ye aught know still your good-before day.

---

1. In Sanskrit guest is called atithi, one without date. Death is also an atithi. A guest visits at whatso date, and none knows when he would leave. Most people are frightened of death, and would do anything to stretch their stay on earth. I always wonder why. Man, as guest here, should rather return at the earliest opportunity, and come back with new garments, new goal, and invigorated.

- Ghazals | 03.05.14 |

Courtesies, then and now

Five hundred years, free-spelling times,
It was when 'pinck of curtesie'[1],
And minstrel 'pauzed for courtezy'[2],
Servile, bend knees, showed 'curtesy'[3],
Deeply bowing, bounden curtsy;
Old-fashioned has now grown— like rhymes,
From free-flowing, free-spell,
Old values when scarce sell.

---

1. Shakespeare in Romeo and Juliet (1592)
2. Unknown author, Shakespeare's contemporary in 1575
3. Yet another spelling during Elizabethan times

Today, spellings are specific. There is no room for a leeway as was in older times. Also, we use courtesy for general politeness, and curtsy for specific. So much precision as is in mechanical tools, and yet, courtesies are old fashioned and rudeness prevails more than ever!

- Ways of words | 05.05.14 |

Epicentres galore!

Pedants fume helpless and seethe with rage,
And linguists surrender shall in age,
Media always misuse
Commoners to confuse,
Quiver not nor quake o'er rage on page!

Perhaps epicentre sounds a bit grander than just centre. Yet, it is used only in context of earth-quakes—the point on the earth above the spot quaking, from epi (Greek), meaning over or above. But media prefer epicentre in all contexts— political, social, economic, any. Pedants and classicists and linguists may quake with anger, or boil with rage. Yet, dictionaries will ultimately capitulate and compromise.

- Ways of words | 06.05.14 |

Where's the face you once knew?

Early morn sleep deprived, and of life,
You oft struggle to get up from bed,
After a late night and heavy head,
It's indeed hard playing spouse to wife.

You carry on still— the same old role,
Convincing or not yet, life's a stage,
Pleasing none, pursuing the same goal,
It gets harder hanging on to hedge.

Rushing as always to work, new tasks,
And spending yet one more thankless day,
Playing and pretending, wearing masks—
One each for every role you aught play.

Playing boss here, an ideal colleague
There, a co-operating team-mate,
And what's most demanding one to fig—
A hard-working hand— still to stagnate!

Comes evening, friends, mates in water holes,
As many faces as there are masks,
Pretending and playing out odd roles—
As many roles as are thankless tasks.

Aniruddha Pathak

Home again, and dying to relax,
The day's done, but shows none of its tail—
To parents you're a son far too lax,
To children, a hold-all hard to hail!

In bath for cool shower
At last, time to be you,
In front of old mirror,
Where's the face you once knew?

- Introspecting | 09.05.14 |

Prayer, no petition for pardon

Ye know, Father, I'm a prodigal son,
Lost in life's litmus tests, left with no fight,
No one hails he whose mind is on the run,
Thine son that feels like a ship sunken,
Drowning, and darkling gets the night;
I know, Lord likes repentant heart and head,
So come I have a straightened countenance,
And made polite in true penitence
For all the mistakes that I've made,
As soldier in the battlefield of life,
I'm here, Lord, for a glimpse, your darshan[1],
And brought have I no petition,
I'll fight my fight till last of breath is rife,
And confident with your grace, my faith,
Unbent, unconquered by fate, till my death.

An ocean art thou of compassion,
I seek alms, nor am pleading my case,
Pitiful sons that plead in vain you shun,
I seek your goodly grace, kindly face,
Only if ye should feel pleased with me,
Crops cultivated I seek to reap,
I know you've given me eyes not to weep,
But yonder horizons to see;
This is my fair and just view,
You're mighty great, agreed,
Yet, your son too is no lowly breed,
Bless me if I deserve to get my due.

You have given the wide world enough,
Wind, water, light, ether and fire,
Sun and Moon, starry skies— entire,
Why, whole cosmos and all useful stuff,
I wonder what to give you, great giver,
Save, try and be your worthy son,
And yet, I'm no one-way receiver,
I'll see that my dues are duly done.

So, Lord, if I come to thee,
Heavens, if 'tis to beg, be happy,
Just that if and when a mistake I make,
My steps waver, slip up or shake,
You'll understand as a good father,
That human I'm, not much farther,
Pray, be no Yama² with a punishing sceptre,
And a list of where I did falter,
Nor be a judge never to pardon,
Be thou a kindly father in my garden.

And I've a prayer on where you dwell,
Pray, let not your palace chief, temple priest,
Make a timetable, and a do's and don'ts list,
And all meaningless minutia on spell,
How can a Lord of world in prison be?
Your true abode is all of heaven;
With feeling heart I come, you to see,
If not friend, let me be a proud son.

---

1. Darshan¹: For His holy sight, a glimpse.
2. Yama²: The Lord of Death.

meet his old friend, but did not talk of his poverty.

Be from false mercy free

If pain in love there's, be from such love free,
'A fulcrum I'm', be from all such whims free.
 Both yes and no do bind— to near and dear,
 Be from fens of anticipations free.
Sticking to which whatso makes little sense,
Be from such dos and don'ts, rules and reins free.
 And gilded dreams of malls that rob the eyes,
 Be from such glares, mirages and mires free.
From ostrich fears and false crocodile tears,
O face life's truth, and be from false truth free.
 Oft wearing heart upon sleeves they meet us,
 Be from such sentimental ho hums free.
And such that ye meet thee at soul's leisure,
Be from soul-less faiths and false mercy free.

Free translation of a Gujarati poem by Mahendra Joshi,
titled, mukta thai ja.

- Ghazals | 02.01.14 |

That's happiness for me

Just a look at her e'er so happy,
She eying a toy to her pleasing,
Playing in mother's lap, and smiling,
Lost in a lullaby ere sleeping,
That's where my happiness haps to be.

Throwing a heavy school-bag aside,
Uniform, homework all else beside,
Or bunking classes— leave un-applied,
Enjoying rain— from every care free,
That is where happiness do I see.

Many a muted dream in her mind,
A tender age in love that be blind,
On the way on a date as ere lined,
Smiles when seeing him there already,
That for sure happiness is for me.

Waking early one day,
She finds house lonely lay,
And door-bell rings up at dawn's first ray,
Her daughter, kids hugging with rare glee,
That is what I call feeling happy.

An old man bent by too tired a back,
Picks up, plays a cassette from old rack,
The sun is preparing when to pack,
Him dancing after long when I see,
That (what else), happiness to me be.

This is translation of a Gujarati poem by *Shyamal Munshi*, titled *mane to sukh emaaj dekhay*. The metre used is anapaest.

- Translations | 03.01.14 |

Temples of God

A tender tree leaf,
Young blades of grass, if
Fail to firm up my belief . . .

- Haikus | 04.01.14 |

All the heft and no height

To inspire each head
God an infinite world made;
Man held on to heft, no height.

- Haikus | 05.03.13 |

My small stature

If trivial should trouble my mind's eyes,
Time it is to shed all my disguise.
Today if things annoy,
By morrows might destroy
Me, wonder it's my esteem's true size.

- Reflections | 01.04.13 |

I laid my heart bare

I laid my heart bare
Seeing starry strings as ere—
But unmoved, blank they still were!

Man feels he is central in nature's scheme of things. But it is time he realizes that it is not so. The world we know does not move around us as we thought earlier. Humans and the whole solar system is an insignificant dot in universe. To heavenly bodies, we count for nothing whatso.

- Haikus | 02.04.13 |

Me, a mere dot

Vast lies vacant world without,
Vast, the space within,
And me in between!

- Haikus | 03.04.13 |

The better side of things

A raging storm that tore up in pace,
Brought down the sun-shed on my terrace;
Brighter sun's now one boon,
Better I see the moon,
Ah blizzard too has a benign face.

- Reflections | 03.07.13 |

Poor pedants packed to trivia

Single file never walked criteria,
Bacteria, nor the word of media;
Bad coins do drive out good,
Truth shrugs in solitude,
And pedants are packaged as trivia.

To talk of 'criteria' as plural, to say 'media' are and not is, to talk of one bacterium and not bacteria is today to attract a stare from a pedant. Today this is truly trivia.

- The ways of words | 11.07.13 |

Hispanic hot Basque

Hitch hiking to Hispanic hot Basque[1]
In north coast, in sunny land to bask,
A man met his muse there,
Basking there— bare with dare,
She wore a bare tight blouse known as basque[2].

Basque[1]: A costal region in Spain; basque[2]: A tight-fitting low cut bodice worn by women of poor repute.

Together with the more common bask, the three words often confuse, which this limerick tries to clear.

- Ways of the words | 04.08.13 |

O to die for belief

Religion, many have for it fought,
Patriots as die for piece of land,
And others for whatso be a cause,
There are some that die world peace to mend.
Socrates the only soul there was
That died for the defence of his thought,
In times when it was torture to think,
Tyranny besides, freedom of thought—
People jumped to act ere eyes could blink,
To think was to scheme, and he was caught.

This small piece is set in anapaest metre, three feet per line.

- Reflections | 02.09.13 |

Who would believe?

If sorrows seem to me joys, who'd believe?
If water were to turn mirage, who'd grieve?
 Drink to drown your sorrows, your woes,
  Was vouched by a worthy sage, who'd believe?
If very lifeline turns to death—
What can save me, who can my pain relieve?
 And when I jumped in to die, I sank not,
 But swam ashore and safe to live!
For, He hailed, helping hands to give,
I seldom can this game of His believe.
 The door where stranger-like I stood
 To brood, was my own, who'd believe?
My ill fame, bad name I did grieve,
It was love's honour received! Who'd believe?

Ghazals come in couplets generally in odd numbers. They have a constant refrain of one rhyme repeating In every couplet. The stanzas are thematically related. Urdu is the language in which Ghazals first originated. This one was inspired by a Gujarati piece of which I no more recall.

- Ghazals | 05.09.13 |

Man only waits

Time waits, nor heavens,
Nor nature whatso happens;
For trifles man waits.

- Haikus | 09.09.13 |

You scarce are common

I oft shooed you, decried as bird bare brain,
You hide behind O bird talent tad rare,
Should someone nurture you and care to train,
Your sense of shades no bird seems to share.

You have a knack to know your trainer's lead—
That's what makes you a bird of choicest breed,
O angel, you 'lone can spot a Monet
From a Picasso, peace pigeon, prized pet!

That's what I saw when with a huge flock, you
Took off from the ground given a command,
O swirling in the sky, thence out of view,
And showing skills in flight, and thence to land;

You trapped when birds of rival fleet—what treat!
And earning thereby a choicest diet—

Of dry fruits and pure cottage ghee wee bit,
And staple food of course, corn and millet.

I never knew doves could be trained to tell
A human voice, a whistle, and many
A hand gesture to return safe and well
To base, until I did your talent see.

You have the measure of magnetic field
Of Earth, I was so told, that you know at best
Spots in uncharted space, your power to wield,
Returning thence spot on to place of rest!

And your eyes have more colour cones than us,
That you can see three times as many shades
O making you a bird so precious,
Shade captured scarce from your memory fades.

O you perennial guest of my lone house,
I'd ne'er shoo you away now that I know
You are not like a pesky pest— the mouse;
Yet, wish some hygiene, good habits ye show!

For, you make every corner, every niche
Of my house your nestling place, what rage!
A maternity home all so hellish,
Ye aught know: house is no home of garhage!

It's odd we call you a common pigeon,
With your credentials scarce art you common.

- Reflections | 03.01.12 |

I recall

To many when a way showed way out,
Alternatives when flowed all around,
Expert minds invented germ of doubt,
Specialists felt, alts were far from sound;
Things when seemed possible to lay-heads,
An expert was red with unknown dreads.

If I were a Tata or a Ford,
I would shun experts, all expertise,
And would have no expert on my board;
One with width, li'le depth, no expert is,
Nor is a closed mind and crooked bent,
Who fears fall, fails to experiment.

I'm all for him that acts and sees yon,
Suggest who can ten alts, one to take,
Treads paths to where no one has ere gone,
Afraid who scarce be errors to make,
Whose eggs hatch not in much-trodden bag,
Theories and books be whose red rag.

For God said, men in doubt vanish would,
Faith in heart he that goes straight ahead,
Carrying with him a thinking head,
A way out is way out, crude or good;
An expert at his best would advise,
One that works with no wired hands is wise.

And world's shy nor short of expert head,
But hands hot, ready to work and red!

I recall how so-called experts and expertise became a virtual fetish in one of the organisations I worked with. I had moved my job-kittens in a few companies and I could get a goodly insight into what would work and what would not. Many companies suffer from experts, who would advise rather than work with bare hands— NATO: No Action Talk Only, and at national level too.

- Tongue-in-cheek | 04.01.12 |

Agony, drops of honey, long journey

A weary way fairer, and lost in wood
One dark night, tired, hungry, fell in a well—
Dry, unused— left him which on fate to brood,
Lucky to clutch on to roots of a swell
Banyan tree, and hanged half awake midway,
Spending the whole night praying for a ray
Of hope, precariously suspended;
And dreamt: he was lifted out, not yet dead,
In times so trying, sole lifeline from blue,
I wonder what man would without dreams do.

He'd ne'er in life awaited morning more,
Which when came, came to spell disaster—
There growled at the well's mouth a mighty tiger,
Who stared, hunger and greed writ all over;
The only way being unknown way down,
Or resting a while; let the tiger go,
But no, he heard a python hissing, brown
And big, tongue twirling, ready to swallow,
Frail lifeline-like roots when began to buck,
When destinies frown, wonder what would luck!

But when his faint vision began to blur,
The tired mind lost when power to think,
He felt a cooling, sticky little stir,
Dripping from nose to lips, to slowly slink
Down to his mouth; but how, how can it be?
A few drops of heavenly sent honey!

Ahead he saw a bear seated aplomb
'Pon a tree branch above, grabbing the comb!
No, his thoughts on destinies were not true,
And life something has to look forward to.

Well, waiting he was ere for dawn to be,
And then, ah hungry mouths to go away,
And now a few chancy drops of honey,
In an eon that was half night, half day!
And it just dawned to him: life like that is,
But a few licks at a time to relish,
And hitches, glitches, catches everywhere,
And yet, options still smile often to tell:
Plights come with pleasure in life howso bare,
Wisdom's to weigh: how long to wait in well!

This poem is allegorical on life's long journey, which by and large littered is with agony, with a few drops of honey here and there. Man lives amid mere hopes of better times.

- Reflections | 05.01.12 |

Birth of Death

Let me narrate how Death came upon Earth,
Said Vyasa to Yudhishthir so shattered
By Abhimanyu's death he wished to die—
'It's me that a young dream now lies scattered'.

A story 'tis of an ancient age—
Of king Akampan that had lost his all
In war— dear son[1] that battles fought so brave,
In a losing cause that had cost him tall.

Lost in grief, short of hope, he wandered 'lone,
Looking in vain to take mind off the war,
And fortunate indeed of fate that he
Met sage Narada, his life's Poll Star.

'My son was brave to face celestial gods,
'Whom gods could not have killed, how can die he?
'Pray tell me what death is, what dying means,
'I know life's fate, what's death's destiny?'

The sage told the story of creation—
Of Birth of Death, of old age and disease:
When Brahma had the cosmos created,
Oh, death had no role in the scheme of His.

And life lived and lived for endless long years,
None died, none left, and new life came to be,
And Earth could scarce ballooning burden bear,

Life was ne'er-waning-e'er-waxing vast sea!
An endless ocean of life in a tide,
Taxing Mother Earth's meagre means, no pause,
And ere long caused chaos, cathartic ill,
Food scarce to fuel millions of hungry maws.

And hard it was to breathe, the Creator
Felt concerned: how to turn the giant tide,
How to lighten the burden borne by Earth,
Ere, crushed by daunting weight, the poor soul died.

Brahma thought for long hours and days on end,
'Poor me, oh how I never thought of this?'
Yet, a way out eluded no less still,
His three heads showed creases where ere was bliss.

In rage His eyes looked like a red hot coal,
And flames of fire flared forth, worlds to consume—
All heavens and solar space yon of Earth,
Looked as if nigh was cosmic night's dour doom!

Gods and goblins sauntered soon to pray,
Earthlings too came earnest, came seers, came peers,
To placate kindly God, easy to plead—
Shiva, folded hands, eyes flooding with tears.

He, sacrifice dwelling in matted locks,
Concerned, compassionate, in common plight,
Volunteered O to plead and pacify
Brahma—to rise to His creative height.

Seeing Shiva with folded hands, said He
Bowing, 'pray do tell me what I should do';

'The Father of this cosmos aught be kind,
'Yet, ye scorch it— the rage ere long you'd rue'.
'No, not enraged am I on creatures mine,
'Nor am I engaged to destroy, O Lord,
'I know not still how to lighten the Earth,
'Let me assure— I'm no punishing rod.'

'I thought for long without succeeding still,
'Frustrated, in dry rage, my eyes flash fire';
'But let not this Creation come to naught',
Said Shiva, 'be thou pleased, relax O Sire'.

'Save these lakes, save rivers, save all thine sons
'And daughters; spare this universal pain,
'Think of a wise way out, and better still—
'How if they die to get born once again?'

'Let Time unto three-fold time zones divide:
'One is what hath come, never to return,
'One that is vast, unknown, not on the ride,
'And present that unfolds— now on the run'.

He hearkened wise and well, three heads of His,
Restrained his rage, recalled his scorching flares,
Absorbed all fire unto eternal bliss,
Of course, let birth and death bear equal shares.

Let humans tread a path one of a twain[1]:
The path of karma—of good deeds, to earn
Fruits, place in heaven, earn and spend in chain;
Or of knowledge—the path of no return.

Brahma created a form female-head,
A thought born of the need, of weird form—

Blue and green from rainbow, tongue and mouth red,
Eyes burning yellow, like a raging storm.
She came to be and stood there facing South,
A tad confused of her cosmic mission,
With smile awaiting a word from Lord's mouth,
Which, when came, came like lightning from heaven.

'Dear daughter, Death art thou, nay, a goodwill,
'Thine mission 'tis to kill all life alive,
'Born art thou of mine rage, and aught thou kill
'Evil and good no less, wise with the naïve'.

So said, poor maid, with a mission to kill,
Began to shed tears springing from deep grief,
Thinking ahead still of mankind's goodwill,
The Lord held forth her copious tears on leaf.

Suppressing her motherly grief, somewhat
Emboldened by Brahma's eternal grace,
She breathed courage if but for a moment,
And shy like creeper said with a kind face:

'O thou of wise words, be graceful to me,
'I wonder why one would want a woman—
'One born by nature kind— to come and kill,
'Kill life, I know not, how I ever can.'

'Scared am I of sin, be graceful to me,
'I scarce can imagine what would the kin
'Of the slain—friends and well-wishers what be—
'Say of this cruel act of mine so mean.'

'I scarce can stand sufferings in the lands,
'But pardon me—thou art my last refuge,

'O Ancestor, I plead with folded hands,
'Not equal I feel to the task this huge.'
'Let me go do long arduous tapas
To please thee'; but the Lord passed His decree:
'Do carry out what thou art born to do,
'Worry not, no evil shall come 'pon thee'.

'Naught much can be done on what ordained is,
'Get on to thine mission, have faith in me,
'Thou shalt incur no sin, my word of bliss,
'Be thou but a trigger of Destiny!'

Poor woman! Kind of heart, called still to kill,
Fains if she could utter a word of will,
Protest, nor ever procrastinate still,
Said yes, nor no, served of a bitter pill.

And slipped away soon from Lord's kind visage,
To a far off hermitage of a sage,
The death goddess performed penance ardent,
Fifteen cosmic years², single foot unbent!

Failing to soften when Brahma's mind still,
She meditated for twenty more years,
And pleaded, 'spare me Lord but I can't kill
Innocent life, nor can stand tainted tears.

This too when failed to move Him, she took to
Deep silence— of thought, speech, and inner soul,
And took to waters³ to moist Brahma's heart;
Said He, 'Life's born to fulfill karmic role'.

'Resist not daughter mine, to me so dear,
'Dharma thine own alone cleanses inner being,

''Divine will shall assist thee; have no fear,
'None shall blame thou for killing life, living'.
'In men thou shalt live as man, as woman
'In women, in life an image of mine;
'Life shall grow old and ill— in flesh and mind,
'Let it conspire to kill in course of time.

And shall get born in a perennial chain,
A new life to live, new body and mind,
O to carry on all over again
The journey, to start from whence left behind.

'I've saved copious tears ye shed at my gate,
'Let them ailments be of many a kind,
'Ill emotions like rage, desire, and hate
'Shall do the trick, and clock's set to unwind.

No bane, Death's boon, and man's greatest of friend,
Creation can't come to be without Death,
As there's no new beginning if no end,
Let Death get born along with life's first breath.

And so was Death born in ancient years,
A boon to life to beget new body,
And to carry on with onward journey,
A young driver, new vehicle, on high gears!

This poem is based on an episode in Mahabharata.

1. pravrutti, path of karma; nivrutti, path of knowledge.
2. Brahman years: The abode of Brahma being light years away 15
    years are to be taken in cosmic terms.

- Epics | 01.06.12 |

Antique is still an asset

A coin that once was gilded,
I was a valued asset,
In currency, well traded;
Now a loose change, rotated
Though, but never much rated;
I wonder oft of my fate—
That with no expiry date,
Is not antique still an asset?

- Tongue-in-cheek | 01.07.12 |

The Waverly Inn

Whitefield, suspended and frozen in time,
A relic of the past, verdant lush green,
Not far away from urban glare and grime;
Nestled in hist'ry was Waverly Inn.

But not ere long it lived in old-world charm,
Alluring what with rare mystique beauty,
Protestant mores— protected well from harm—
From a bustling big brother city;

Its neo Gothic church— century old,
Trellis wooden cottages blending well
Rich with relics under its ample fold,
Rosewoods, English crockery, dunk old smell!

And a rotund romantic interlude
O hidden at archives in dusty hood.

Whitefield, near Bangalore, a settlement more than a century old is nestled in history and Nature. Eurasians and Anglo-Indians lived there. It boasted of Whitefield Club famous for ball-room dances. Many fell in and out of love there, a fall out of the dances. But today the old charm is fast vanishing what with multi-storied malls, new things and the hustle and bustle of the Sai Baba ashram. Though the place has now turned cosmopolitan, many cling to memories, make-believe world.

1. Survived still has this Waverly Inn there that witnessed a conquest[1] not recorded by history. Winston Churchill used to frequent this Inn to court the daughter of innkeeper James Hamilton. A fact few might believe. But 'unknown to most he was an incorrigible romantic', says Michael Shelden in his recent book 'Young Titan: The Making of Winston Churchill'. The new generation is still being regaled here with claims that the place has been the relic of romance— a rock with the initials WSC engraved in a heart, Cupid's arrow passing through it.

- Relics from far | 01.08.12 |

Ode on old virtues

Virtue, O rare old wine of vague value
Admired today by vintners nary more,
Nor partakers; time has taken its cue,
Bad boasts, try to be good, good hides indoor.

Watch thou achievers surfacing from shores—
Evil, looking chic, tonnes pouring in offers,
Take Tiger Woods—no more now in good roars,
Still roars, backed by millions in the coffers!

If they were no manic odd men and out,
Would Mark be such a Face he is today?
Would biggies of big screen be such a clout?
Would scandal-prone leaders rule the poor lay?

Achievements arrive on no efforts lean,
Yet, can't wipe out a single sorry trait,
Nor may success come to purest Brahmin,
But commerce and big bucks make biggest bait.

And flavours get spread 'pon many a field:
Be it movies, business, brands, even books,
Money's the recipe that whatso cooks,
And repute may from worst of ruins rebuild.

Actors are made and unmade by last hit,
Best sellers 'lone can take authors to crest,
Dough drives it all backed by evilest grit,

Old values stare in face of men modest.
Few can recall a Mensa topping boy,
Who does not the five crore KBC[1] man?
Money when sings the world dances in joy,
Bad-plus-big-bucks be the new dung-hill hen.

Let me not play tuneless in today's time,
Some purists do get praised with Gandhian,
Yet, crass nevertheless is no more crime,
And old values are hailed but in heaven.

And whilst weighing values for weathered time,
Let's mull on what Greeks[2] said: Thou shouldst secure
Safe income ere vouchsafing virtues pure;
So wisdom always weighed, not value-rhyme.

Some go for health, power, or reach for riches,
Honours, to some touch of pleasure pleases,
Few if any place in virtues chief good[3];
Heart may value virtues, head wearing hood.

Gravity's one, and magnanimity,
Earnestness, kindness, and sincerity,
To confuse more, clear less, came Confucius[4]
Who defined what virtue aught be to us.

And holy cows at a premium are sold,
Why virtue as a species has gone rare,
In a world that today wallows in gold
Standard, market's driven by a dark mare!

Old values, whilst you may vouch worlds of good,
Old prayers of virtue, in silence said,

Can conquer not the world Lao-tse laid²;
Clueless and confused I retire to brood.
And digging deep into an ancient text—
Mahabharata, a storehouse of lore,
In today's times still knee deep in context—
It tried, failed fixing dharma— root and core.

Failed author Vyasa fully to define,
Failed Bheeshma, a man no one could well size,
Man of truth Yudhishthir; Vidur, the wise,
All it managed was, 'dharma is divine'!

Yet, there seems but one thing to me nigh clear:
Virtues and vice, the twain of twain so tall,
Alone survives death, sailing with soul;
So let me virtues cheer, my vices fear!

Or in today's times going in fifth gear,
I should my virtues fear, my vices cheer!

---

1. KBC: Popular Indian TV show, Kaun banega crore-pati?,
2. Anonymous Greek saying: 'First secure an independent income, and then practice virtue.'
3. From what Marcus Tullius Cicero said on friendship.
4. 'Five things constitute perfect virtue: gravity, magnanimity, earnestness, sincerity, and kindness.' - Confucius.
5 'With virtue and quietness one may conquer the world,' - Lao-tse: The Simple Way.

- Ode, Satire | 09.08.12 |

My date with Death

Seeing Death, eye in front, in rear,
And squatting at my front door,
I get alarmed— not with fear,
And wish him well as before;
Wish welfare of my known guest—
If he's tired, would like to rest.
At times he nods, comes in, and
Even warmly shakes my hand,
Suggesting while still smiling:
We should spend more time meeting.

I oft think of meeting you,
I say, friendship to renew,
But scarce am alone, you see,
Surrounded with so many:
Eyes and ears, my poking nose,
Tongue and this skin always close;
Seeking am a solitude
To do my soul long-missed good;
Moment I find me alone,
In touch with true me and none,
Haply no doubt I'll ye meet,
Open arms and soul to greet,
I know not when that can happen,
Nor that moment wait from heaven.

Based on a poem in Gujarati by Hareendra Dave

-Translations | 11.08.12 |

Beauty

Wrapped in layers as is onion,
Some say, beauty's an opinion.
Had it been heftier a fact,
Beauty would be far more perfect;
Berthed in beholder's biased eyes,
Singing of holder's eyes it lies;
What holds me is love eyes emit,
To which her heart 'hind I credit,
That may be a mere opinion
Cast off as layers of onion,
Yet, layer no less onion is,
As is man opinion of his!

- Tongue-in-cheek | 02.09.12 |

Madhavas on river Mahi²

I well remember Madhavas¹ still,
A water-hole to unwind in sweltering June,
From crusty book-fields to dusty farm-fields,
And do-nothings from morn to mid-night's noon!

And how we arrived in a bullock cart,
Moving in matching tune with speed of night,
All of eight odd miles from my town,
To reach as dark kissed dawn goodnight.

I was one amid a cart-load
Of kids; others around sleepy,
My sleep hijacked by stars, planets,
Who too excited seemed like me.

The oxen pair called each to each,
The cart-man when cleared his dry throat,
The stars too tired when went to sleep,
We reached— wrapped with a dusty coat.

Soon when I heard a bird singing
Close by, proclaiming reign of dawn,
A few more birds called confirming,
In symphony they welcomed new-born morn.

Once there I meet my friend Mahi²
That charmed my forebears to choose this village,
Flowing bank to bank all seasons,
Some memories get frozen in image.

Harvest of the Late Season

The river was why village was,
Whose life along its waters flowed,
From pre-bath chores and all-after,
Swim and loiter till sun to zenith strode.

And felling of choicest mangoes
My month-long pass-time was,
Men guarding fields the only foes,
And roaming lush green fields, no pause!

When one month passed like one short turn,
Day, but a song 'tween sun's rise and set;
And soon it was time to return
To tired routine by elders set, no let.

A lot gets lost when from tired mind,
How I remember Madhavas[1] for so long?
We live and leave a lot far behind
Yet, deeply-etched freeze childhood's cherished song.

Madhavas[1]: A small village in west-central hills of Gujarat.

Mahi[2]: Also known as Mahi Saagar, one of the biggest, perennial rivers in Gujarat.

- Nostalgia | 03.09.12 |

Kadamb's

When I her see so close from my terrace,
Swaying in joy, embracing nearby trees,
Her grey leaves falling off from greener grace,
With every burst of balmy monsoon breeze,
Pale ones waiting to fall in resigned ease,
And wonder how if one learns: life's on lease—
Endless patience of trees, wet spell or son,
E'er bowing to the will of wide Nature,
In tune with time, to mood of the season,
To stand triumphant still with tall stature;
And admiring from far, somewhat nigh cool,
I always stand a student of its school.

There's something peculiar about all rains,
It does strange things to me, to trees alike;
It's not water— elixir though of life,
(They draw it through the roots and leaves from air,
But rains seem special to all greens, know not how,)
While watering my plants I see they smile,
And still worry on over-watering,
Having seen them suffer a decayed death,
Yet, I see weeds growing on sheer self-will,
Rains stretching their green smile an extra mile;
But trees seem to take rains in their firm stride,
And none the worse for Nature's largesse seem.

And in a few days I see what rains do:
Kadamb[1] has come to spell its monsoon spell,
Under many a green leaf hangs a fruit
Growing, many still far too small to see,
Some heading the race, showing off their plume,
A yellowish orange coat of young buds,
Like furs of a tennis ball, blossoming
All around the fruit's glistening surface;
There follows soon a swarm of honey bees,
And variety of sprightly butterflies,
Feasting in a spell in undisturbed ease,
And feast no less to my un-tired old eyes;
Good seldom lasts long still, a fact of life,
Kadamb[1] gets no grace from Nature's wise rule.

The orange furs ripen soon to acquire
A darkling brown shade to fall on the ground
Below, in a smooth bed-spread all around,
Much like Parijaat flowers from heaven,
And yet no match to their heady fragrance;
Buds die as buds, ere blossoming to smile.
The bald fruit, a smallish tennis ball now,
Soon ripens to attract Simian brigades,
Making me wonder, why humans avoid
Them at all— wonderful in look no less,
And tempting as I see from my far shore;
Yet, there's no word in ancient Indic lore
That Krishna playing there cherished the fruit,
He spent though years of his childhood and more,
Cavorting with young maids, playing cane flute,
But I'm always tempted to try the fruit.

Kadamba¹ sheds leaves, growing new through the year,
Not in autumn alone, a wiser thing
To do in my ill-informed wisdom though;
But spring has come, a bedecked youthful bride,
Inviting ace singers therein to hide,
Calling a matching mate from unknown far,
Vigorous note, the fifth constant does call,
A heavy heart sings ever more intense;
And oft I feel a note of frustration,
The call fails when to get a counter call,
But most city birds, now a thinning lot,
Should better know, not just bipeds alone,
Birds too pay for progress the time as moves.

A few more birds come and go thro' the day,
Nesting amid brick-made wood's niches, nooks,
Doves seem to have fully abandoned trees,
Others seem wary of men, but this night's
Sole dweller hanging on it upside down—
The bat— the black guest of the darkling night,
Who chooses to vacate ere dawn is bright.

But I, in life's grey evening solitude,
Sitting in a corner of my terrace,
Sipping tea of satisfaction, thinking
Of life that had been— a much trodden wood,
Of chunks of chafing course of little grace,
Ah, day-dreaming acquiring an odd wing,
Yet, mind coming back to this Kadamb¹ tree:
All buds never blossom to be a flower—
As every monsoon cloud seldom does shower—

To fall off ere time, loamy mix to be;
But every single bee, each butterfly,
O makes my age still worth living well nigh.

Kadamba[1]: Encephellous Kadambus, the trees are of two main varieties found in India, one native, the other a close cousin.

Set largely in blank verse in iambic penta-metre. But as the narrative part of the poem becomes reflective, as in the first and the last stanzas, the lines acquire rhymes and are no more blank.

- Reflections | 04.09.12 |

Cants of a canting world

O to walk unrepentant, head held high, unbent,
Righteous or not when be your stakes,
Pretending to break bread with poor whilst eating cakes—
Bread as an ideal insurance,
And cake a hound that with hares runs—
And pompous paying tithes disguised as cant.

We live in an age whose soul is all shades of cant—
Callous to core, yet all correct,
For, none, all age, is made perfect,
My walking straight makes little dent
To time's spirit unrepentant,
I'm no fish against flow to swim, nor act.

Take to sham-faced philosophy, or learn
Poetic lines a tad too tame,
Use ad lib moral cants; to turn
Turtle on head is no more shame,
Nor are shame double-distilled lies
That devil well honed to no one's surprise.

Cants, meaningless noughts on their own,
Made of base metal shining like pure gold,
And multiplied many a fold,
Trailed by a decimal numeral of renown;
Ah, what would world do without cants!
If devil for his labours gets no rents!

Harvest of the Late Season

The lord gave a message of modesty
To man— to live a life of lent,
He, biting apple for times too many,
E'er since hides shame hind a fig-leaf nigh scant,
Taking twelve hours of fast, twelve long to feast,
One month of Lent, the rest for cant and twist!

- Tongue-in-cheek | 08.09.12 |

All don'ts into do's

There comes a man defeated in his mind,
Unsure like a dog— tail tucked to the hind,
And what was an opportune open door,
O looks like unreachable far off shore.
He goes thro life as if led, of no alts,
Chasing mirages, serving double-faults!

Comes then a man with great belief in him,
Walking a lion's gait, musing on dream,
And what ere was a door closed shut on face,
Looks to him a sure shot— a tennis ace,
All odds-against to nil, serving on deuce,
A winner to vantage, don'ts into dos!

"To a pessimist, his opportunities look like difficulties. To an optimist, the difficulties are like opportunities."

- Reflections | 10.09.12 |

What can be better than that?

My life's river if be in spate,
What can I want still more than that?
If someone loves me to this date,
What can I want still more than that?

If one comes to my life like rain,
Bringing a pleasant smell of earth,
What more still can I wish to gain?
There's li'le in world of greater worth.

Darkling clouds have spread all around—
In heavens, all along the ground,
And someone comes like sun shining,
What's better than this silver lining?

One is on verge his life to end,
A stranger comes like long-lost friend,
On a mission a life to mend,
What's better than this helping hand?

Amid many a pen as mine,
If you still read till my last line,
What wonder I can better be?
Nigh else can make me more happy.

Translation of a Gujarati piece by Kiransimh Chauhan

- Ghazals | 01.10.12 |

Aniruddha Pathak

Of Banyan trees and river banks

Until sixth century since Christ came,
Known it was still by the ancient name,
Vatapatrak[1] – leaf of Banyan tree,
Born on banks— river Vishvamitree,

Invited I was O from heaven[2],
By a self-made-Brahmin of same name,
For Ashram hands' holy ablution,
Such was my heritage, such my fame.

To my bank settled a busy town,
Ankottka[3], born of a well-known tree,
A small settlement of huge renown,
That traded with Romans across sea.

Centuries and handsome has it hone,
Claiming in many ways self-renown,
Yet the tree that the town her name gave,
Nigh but lost her roots though fighting brave.

Town fathers did nigh me to protect,
Save soiling my holy flow sublime,
A cancer called growth plundered my prime,
Trees hinder growth they felt, failed to act.

They know not, and let me give this hint:
One Banyan equal is to ten trees,
So blest be her big breath, life's footprint,

Bare-handed can Banyan carbon seize.
Peepal[4], Neem[4], too have a place in sun,
All them be givers of Oxygen,
Yet, Banyans be the sovereign kings,
History many an old lore[3] sings.

In hundreds still they were done to death[6]
In short years of men's mad signature,
Killing me, my town short of fresh breath,
Yet, I hope of good days, green nature.

My old face has scarce been the river,
Nor yet Banyan tress— the name giver
The ancient town no more does breathe fair,
And three of us crave indulgent care.

---

1. Vatapatrak goes back in history to 600 AD ('Leaf of Banyan tree' in Sanskrit). In course of time it became Vada-patrak, and then Vadodara {vada-udara (Belly of Banyan tree}, the British called it Baroda, and in Hindi, Badauda.

2. Sage Vishvamitra created this river for his hermitage (See Mahabharata, Aadi Parva # 71.29/30). In ancient times the river was known as Kaushikee. (Well, river Koshee also claims to be ancient Kaushikee).

3. Ankola or Ankota is erazhil tree (Alangium hexapetalum). Today's Akota was in course of time shortened from this, which still is a western suburb of Baroda. Two thousand years ago it traded with the Romans, A bronze jar handle with a figure of Greek god of love, Eros, pieces of bronze trefoil amphorae, red polished sprinkler and terracotta seals of a European style would testify to these links. People of Akota lived in burned-brick houses. The town was for many years situated as the junction of two major trade roots: one between Ujjain and Bhrigu-kaccha

(the present-day Bharuch; and another between Udaipur and Bhrigu-kaccha, a major port town then.

4. Peepal tree is known as ashvattha in Sanskrit. Neem has high place in Indian Ayurveda. Charaka has sung paeans of praise for it.

5. There were still 1200 Banyan trees in Baroda in 2006. Only but 800 of them were left by 2010.

6. There are a few hopeful signs. GSFC, a public sector fertiliser company in Gujarat has grown some 150,000 Banyan trees in her factory premises and elsewhere. Allahabad, Kanpur, Varanasi, and Bangalore are also known to have a sizeable population of these trees. With their green foliage and huge spread, they can be virtual lungs for a polluted place.

- Nostalgia | 04.04.11 |

Power from cave to grave

Man's always paddled to powerful and strong,
Worshipped what to his wishes would not yield,
Commanded the weak-kneed, committed wrong,
From days of braves, barbarian battlefield,
Power from caves and crannies, counting till grave,
O on pretext of principles to save.

He that rises to heights of stratosphere,
He that holds on power to his heart so dear,
Afraid of honest peer, living in fear
Of losing, scared that laws would interfere,
Afraid, the flow of power may interrupt,
To him, an easy prey, power shall corrupt.

In today's scene— caps in coveted house,
Where polling polls may anoint them to rule,
Hallowed that look in chair like harmless cows,
But behave like bulls, wield every power tool,
And ready soon pilfered power to disburse,
Ah cronyism sprouting from tax-paid purse.

And each power cap a poisonous creature,
Each wielding an exaggerated view
Of him though power's like an early dawn's dew,
Each grabs till grave, each sinks to his stature,
Still crying out like starving babes— 'give, give',
A hungry maw knows not but to receive.

But we that glibly put power to hell-hands—
Turbid hands of a power-hungry tyrant,
Rare if cavil, turn would they faceless fiends,
To prove unworthy of the trust ere lent,
Nor wonder why a facile face should frown,
A beggarly bent face that once looked down!

We that should well know power's every pitfall,
That unbridled power should sooner vanish,
Go to push up the same Peter and Pall,
And long as power prevails rulers and ruled
Shall be, and so shall be shahs and slavish,
Their very tools exploiting facile fools!

We that know, power is rooted down from mind,
Roots out humane gentle virtue— scarce vice,
Greater the power, greater the grab behind;
But voters scarce beware, a loaded dice
Decides; diamonds that dazzle always strike—
Beholders no less than holders alike!

Dignifying the meanest of the means,
Magnifying midgets of smallish mind,
Deigning dignity to damnedest of scenes,
The lowly in exalted chairs are lined,
If power can intoxicate best of hearts,
I shudder what it can to mere warts.

And laws are laid power to perpetuate,
In statute does lay supine power's last cue,
Let majority that acquiesce not wait,
To stall the slavery of week-kneed few;
Power per se seldom should corrode like rust,

What does is her in-sin-born child called lust.
Beware; no power concedes without clamour,
It watches if people submit to more,
To know what more unjust wrongs to lever,
And would last till resisted, words or war;
Like loyalty to land lasts a short spell,
It's rare— wisdom and power marry and well.

Beware O much-ruled man, the strong ne'er lust
For power; rooted it is in weak unjust;
If human mind prone to pride is without,
How much more would it be with more in clout!
If man's power-admiring vainest of toad,
'A slave in mind loves tyrannical ode'.

He is the power-providing ready plug,
A parent raising corruptible child,
Now bribing gift, now letting pass a drug,
Under a cool nose are grave habits piled;
Indulges he till spreads the pestilence,
And child keeps taxing parental patience.

As is an off-switch-less power to a prince,
Wine and woman, to bull as be red rag,
As bribe to bureaucrat has been long since,
Avarice to old age, musk to the stag,
Vanity to vain, to greed gratis grant,
To passionate, power-lust is most fragrant.

- Ode to power | 03.05.11 |

A pot of nectar was when woman's womb

Times were when women were valued o'er men,
Whilst beasts of sacrifice always were male,
Farm's stock of cattle were ever female,
And hatcheries supplied were but by hen.

The womb over all else did when matter,
Be it the west or east, past or present,
And likened was to pot-full of nectar[1]
In life that always was immortal meant.

The tree of life— any family tree—
Would wither dry without fertile women,
Who, merged unto families as rivers in sea,
And more precious were than mightiest men.

Though sheltered was she from battles on hand,
She oft played still a virtual woman shield[2],
And history replete for long does stand,
Anywhere in world that women can build.

Vyasa was but a seed-supplying sage,
His sons carrying on Puru lineage,
So were gods, whom Kunti summoned for seed,
Her five sons shared one wife, one each to breed.

Harvest of the Late Season

Parashuram, an ancient brave warrior priest,
Was out when cruellest of kings to rid,
One, king Balik[3], behind womenfolk hid,
O to duck death and breed much like a beast.

The Greek, Achilles, was raised in girly guise,
Safe from warlords itching to battle Troy;
Sword and spear revealing female disguise,
He fought and won— O this dresst-as-girl boy.

But things have turned full round in today's times,
The shield that once saved men faces male crimes,
O weary wombs thou once were female founts,
But passive partners passion when man haunts.

Go look within, O brute sex, if ye can,
Would ye have survived still without women?

- Satire | 03.07.11 |

At sixty four

At sixty four, still learning bare to walk,
At sixty four and well behind the clock,
When freedom daily reels under assault,
Rulers when feel we have salt nor yet alt.

We call us free, painted caps still in lead,
Decide what we should watch not, what not read;
When pizzas get parcelled home red at once—
Much faster than can arrive ambulance;

When car loans easier, quicker can come
Than for studies— in so modest a sum;
When easy comes a reserved quota seat,
Which, merit-listed names never can beat;

When multiplexes, malls take less than year,
Roads and bridges taking long years to clear;
Lemon juice is flavoured artificial,
Dish-wash liquids when claim 'tis quite real;

When people spend tonnes on luxurious rents,
Yet spare money, nor space for old parents;
When 'coolies' and 'caretakers'—dollar-paid,
Sneeze at blue-collars at home as low grade;

Harvest of the Late Season

When first few words upon a road-rage slam
Scarce 'sorry' be, but 'do ye know who I'm?'
When done thing 'tis a grand tour overseas,
And spots at home are: 'local, no, no please';
We keep electing when faces unfair,
And keep trying useless creams to look fair;
With pride we claim Kamasutra to be sane,
Yet throw away our made at home Hussain;

Marriages we claim are when heaven-made,
Twain of young hearts on run while we de-head;
A dry State beats when records of the wet,
Prohibition walks a favourite pet;

When women worshipped are with fervent faith—
Mothers, goddesses, and placed in high dome,
They live a second-class status at home,
Harassed no less, oppressed, banished ere breath;

Many caps enduring power, so inure,
Even fodder as a scam has its lure,
When what one stands for little heft carry,
Gandhi glory gets from Gandhigiri;

Civil servants, oh servants nor civil,
Play dons, but dance at a minister's vile will;
When being late, e'en absent, is no crime,
Being in time, no more a virtue prime!

431

When at sixty four few are liberate,
Fifteenth of August is a one more date,
Less august a day O to dedicate,
A date perhaps to blame us for our fate!

Pray, magic of India lay wisdom is,
Celebration of freedom, if ye please,
And what at stake is to us precious,
Our soul's very spirit that makes us, us!

- On 15th August, Satire | 06.08.11 |

A date with ducks

Comes the mom comb duck crackling,
Her brood behind following—
All of them chicks seventeen,
Ah marvellous wetlands scene.

In fresh-water swamps—to breed,
'Together' seems your sole creed,
Dispersing in wet season,
In swamps in scorching hot sun!

I like, Knob-billed, your common creed:
Seen you in large flocks of hundred,
No leader whoso yet to lead,
And pecking order, tail nor head!

A few things, pray, to men teach—
They that stick to chairs like leech,
Proud frogs, crackling rooster cocks,
They that can't foster their flocks!

On swampy greens 'lone you feed,
Along sturdy water weeds,
On smaller fish, sundry seeds,
You with young chicks, you in lead!

I admire how life you lead,
Happy with girth without greed—
Yet to see but one of you lean—

I love your blue tinge with green.
Who call you ugly duckling?
Beauty there's in white and black,
One thing perhaps you still lack,
The way you sing— coarse crackling.

With feathers black, body white,
And hints of dark blue and green,
A speckled neck, greyish quite,
Your claws a peace prize should win—

Webbed claws— for hunt nor fight made,
Nor your beak, aggression shows,
White gloss, blue-green tinge, no red,
None— hunting or harming knows.

As mom you seem considerate,
On your own your eggs incubate,
And raise chicks single-hand, alone,
All seventeen or more you own.

Comb duck, or knob-billed duck (Sarkidiornis melanotos), an unusual pan-tropical bird is found in tropical wetlands of sub-Saharan Africa, Madagascar, and South Asia from Pakistan to Laos and extreme South China. For facts, courtesy: Bird Conservation Society- Gujarat (BCSG).

- Nature | 11.08.11 |

Poetic tips

A piece gets done when penned and pinned—
Poorly or well, hailed or hollered,
To have tried is not to have sinned.

Good ones oft get born from no good,
Poor one better than one not ran,
Get started, be it childish crude.

A poet, howso good or great,
Has poor poems penned sans number,
Best of bards oft from bad create.

It helps to have some theme of heft—
Love's one, as is death, destiny,
Canvas vast, little need be left.

Beware, heftier be the theme,
Deeper lie devils of details,
From bottom surfaces fine cream.

No pen need nuts and bolts explain,
So, say your say ere you fine tune,
Few readers weigh your labour's pain.

Poetic forms, mere crutching aid,
So, learn to walk with and without,
Discard them soon as shackles dead.

A poet more paints an image

That walks miles, words while strut on stage,
But weaken with passage of age.

A poet has a heart— his own,
And it aches quite unlike any,
Beware of heads O meddle-prone.

A piece with no title to head,
And much like a nameless lost child,
Lazily fathered, dies— not dead.

A poem's born off thought; your pen
And blank paper together paint,
And muse has no use— eight of ten.

Woods are fine, any a place good,
Let thoughts create— heart over head,
An island helps—of solitude.

A limerick, dirty or dull,
A good fun is and a good try,
Perilous looms a longish lull.

Alliteration, a good aid,
Easily O gets overdone,
Let it not dance upon your head.

A perfect line in a long spell,
It does make it well worth a while,
Yet, let not rest be a dry well.

Kiss not away your private shame,
Nor keep worst of demons off page,
Keep honest pen within prime frame,

And send your babes to the wide world,
If to put head and heart to test,
Cage is no place for a free bird.

Poetic lines do easy flow,
Putting the pea in perfect pod,
Slog, nor struggle, no shame to slow.

If not a good one, nor yet great,
Each can a better poet be,
Heed not to head; let heart 'lone let.

No promenade on a paved way,
A poem's new path to explore,
And never too long nowhere stay!

Here are some poetic tips set as Sicilian tersest. Like beauty tips poetic tips too do not always work. These guidelines are still passed on. They were early on passed on to me. To be frank, many represent the mistakes I committed and even do so now. But poets are ruled by hearts, and heart is prone to make mistakes. I have not learnt much from them but hope is: others will. As one ruled more by heart and not head, feel free to break any rule, for heart knows no rule.

- Reflections | 01.10.11 |

Ah, eat the apple and still hoard!

Look unto Nature's entire range,
Its mighty law is change-less change,
Change is king, none of a crowned king,
Progress is autumn, fall and spring.

Open up, soon shall thine life change,
Buddha's said, look for rainbow's range
Of wisdom; and I wished to change,
But it was no mean a challenge.

Should ye like not, go 'head, change it,
If you can't, change the way you think,
If not, there still are ways— to wit,
Wait, change it'll, if not in a wink.

Not whatso in this world endure,
The world might change the way I want—
A Buddhist way the world to cure,
Or, to a changed me naught would haunt.

And never weep that world changes,
For reason there's if it does not,
If there's changeless state, stony ease,
Yet, e'en a stone is in change caught.

Harvest of the Late Season

And birth of a brazen new truth
Mischief brings if not mighty heave;
An agent of change, if not youth,
Let me no axe 'pon feet receive.

Things change, and we change more than things,
Old order change, yielding to new,
Change of habit irks, lay and kings,
Hope mints new order from tired view!

And progress, a two-edge old sword,
Preserves order amid all change,
Amid change-less change preserves change;
Ah, eat the apple and still hoard!

This piece depicts conflict in man though in a lighter tone. It uses some well-known quotes in a twisted way.

-Tongue-in-cheek | 05.12.11 |

Hello winter

In farthest of the far off lands,
From whence Polar edge bends,
Two friends in fair climes sat in sun,
One talked of a worse winter season:
The frost some days so frigid is,
Words no sooner spoke die to freeze,
And unheard for long spells remain,
Ah, tied in knots of snowy chain,
To thaw but when summer months wake,
O audible in year to make.

Ye may keep frost your pompous norm,
But just one kind word I've oft seen,
O that warms up chilliest scene,
Even keep six winter months warm.
Winter at world's end mighty frosty is,
Only to those with no warm memories!

- Tongue-in-cheek | 09.12.11 |